LEGAL
AID
WEALTH

Legal Aid Wealth

◆

Surviving & Thriving On The Salary Of A Public Interest Attorney

JANINE A. SCOTT, ESQ.

AUTHOR'S NOTE: This book is designed to provide competent and reliable information regarding the subject matter covered. However, it is sold with the understanding that the author is not engaged in rendering legal, financial, or other professional advice. Laws and practices often vary from state to state and if legal or other expert assistance is required, the services of a professional should be sought. The author specifically disclaims any liability that is incurred from the use or application of the contents of this book.

While the author has made every effort to provide accurate telephone numbers and Internet addresses at the time of publication, the author does not assume any responsibility for errors or for changes that occur after publication.

Copyright © 2009 by Janine A. Scott, Esq.

Library of Congress Control Number:		2009901437
ISBN:	Hardcover	978-1-4415-1140-9
	Softcover	978-1-4415-1139-3

All rights reserved. No part of this book may be reproduced or transmitted in any form or by any means, electronic or mechanical, including photocopying, recording, or by any information storage and retrieval system, without permission in writing from the copyright owner.

This book was printed in the United States of America.

To order additional copies of this book, contact:
Xlibris Corporation
1-888-795-4274
www.Xlibris.com
Orders@Xlibris.com
56679

CONTENTS
$ $ $ $

Acknowledgments 9

Introduction 11
   My Personal Journey to Financial Independence and Prosperity

Chapter 1 19
   Managing Student Loan Debt:
   Tackling That Five-Hundred-Pound Gorilla

Chapter 2 36
   Identifying Values and Creating Financial Goals:
   Deciding What Matters Most

Chapter 3 43
   Developing a Spending Plan: Moving to Action

Chapter 4 57
   Saving for Retirement: Securing Your Financial Future

Chapter 5 76
   Buying and Owning a Home: Attain the American Dream

Chapter 6 87
   Eliminating Credit Card Debt: Get Out of the Debt Trap

Chapter 7 101
   Handling Financial Setbacks: Don't Give Up

Conclusion 107
   Cultivating an Attitude of Gratitude

This book is dedicated to my parents, Monica and Norman Scott and to my grandmother, Veronica Henry

ACKNOWLEDGMENTS
$ $ $ $

I would like to thank Brigitt Thompson who provided invaluable support and encouragement when this book was just merely an idea. All the feedback that you supplied for my manuscript helped to develop my confidence as a writer. Thank you for giving me the courage to DREAM BIG!

Many thanks go to Hannah Lieberman for critiquing my manuscript and providing me with a unique perspective in the development of this book. Your commitment to legal services is what drives me to do the work that I do as a public interest attorney.

I would be remiss if I did not thank Charles Wynder, Jr. for the positive response and advice given in support of this book.

I am deeply grateful to the following authors who took time out of their busy schedules to meet with me and provide me with much-needed advice so that this book could become a reality: William T. Kerr, Paul Sandler, Kris Shepard, Steven M. Selzer, and Joe Surkiewicz.

I would like to thank the Honorable David W. Young for giving me my first job out of law school to serve as your law clerk and for being my mentor throughout my legal career.

Finally, my utmost respect and admiration goes to Mr. Wilhelm Joseph, Executive Director of the Maryland Legal Aid Bureau, Inc., for your visionary leadership and commitment to providing quality legal services for the poor.

INTRODUCTION
$ $ $ $

My Personal Journey to Financial Independence and Prosperity

Are you tired of riding on a financial roller coaster? Are you getting dizzy from your spiraling debt? Do you want to save money to achieve your dreams and heart's desires? Would you like to be able to handle unexpected bills while being able to meet your day-to-day expenses? Wouldn't it be nice if you could do it all on the salary of a public interest attorney? Well, I am here to tell you that you can! I am living proof that you are not only able to survive but thrive on a public interest attorney's salary. This book will show you how it can be done. However, before I do that, let me tell you a little bit about myself.

When I was in undergraduate school, I majored in accounting. Like most students who were in business school, the goal was to land a lucrative job. I had wanted to make big money so that I could buy a fancy car, get a nice apartment, and go clothes shopping. The thought of helping others and gaining personal fulfillment in my work was the farthest thing from my mind. My goal was to lavish myself with the best, and the only way to do that was to pursue employment at a prestigious corporation. Period!

I had the opportunity to work, every summer during my college years, in the accounting division of a Fortune 500 company. Compared to my friends, who were working at the local shopping malls, I was making a significant amount of money. However, there was a problem. I found my work very boring. Most days, I would sit and stare at the clock wishing for the day to be over. Poring through various spreadsheets did not appeal to me at all. The only day that I looked forward to was payday and what I was going to do with the money when I cashed that check. After a while, the sole goal of making money had started to lose its appeal. As I neared graduation, I began to question whether working in a field that I didn't think would be satisfying was worth it after all.

When I graduated from college, I worked as a financial analyst for a large corporation. As I expected, I did not like the work at all. So I decided to apply to law school. I had taken a few legal courses in college, which sparked an interest in law.

The thought of becoming a lawyer began as I learned about the variety of things I could do with a law degree. However, I did not want to switch my career goals until I was sure. When I decided, at age twenty-two, to change careers and leave the accounting profession to become a lawyer, I vowed that things would be different. My motivation would not be focused solely on money but on a meaningful and fulfilling career where I could make a difference in the lives of others. I wanted to have a high quality of life and, for me, that included both my personal and professional time.

For a long time, I have heard countless people state how they cannot stand their jobs yet continue to work in dead-end positions that suck the very life out of them—just because of the money. By the time they are willing to face the reality that their job does not provide any satisfaction, they have gigantic mortgage payments, hefty car notes, and huge credit card debts. Needless to say, they feel trapped in their jobs and believe they have no choice but to stay put in a dead-end career and deal with it. I did not want that to be my fate in life. So I decided that I was going to focus on doing work that I love with the hope that money would, in some way, follow.

When I entered law school at Syracuse University in 1994, I took the standard first-year law school courses: torts, contracts, property, constitutional law, etc. I scrutinized each class to determine whether that particular area of law was something that I could enjoy practicing when I become an attorney. I took a variety of courses in my second and third year in law school because I wanted to use this opportunity to decide on an area of concentration. Ultimately, I narrowed my interest down to family law and immigration law.

I knew that I wanted to work in the Maryland/Washington DC area. For undergraduate school, I attended the University of Maryland at College Park, fell in love with the area, and knew, at some point, I would return to live there permanently. Finding work in either the area of family law and immigration law was very difficult. There weren't many large law firms in Maryland that had a family law practice. Additionally, jobs in the immigration area that I was interested in were primarily offered through the U.S. Department of Justice Program, which was very competitive.

I never got an offer with the U.S. Department of Justice Immigration Division, but a Syracuse alumnus, who lived and worked in Maryland, suggested that I apply for a judicial law clerkship position. These clerkships were typically one-year positions working for a circuit court judge. This, he advised, would allow me to obtain invaluable work experience and become connected with members of the Maryland bar and judiciary. This was by far the best advice that I received, which subsequently led me to an absolutely fulfilling career and fabulous life as a public interest lawyer.

I applied for several clerkship positions in the Baltimore and Southern Maryland areas. Ultimately, I received and accepted an offer to work for a Baltimore City Circuit Court judge in 1997. That was probably the best career move I made coming fresh out of law school.

The judge for whom I clerked took an interest not only in my career as a young lawyer but also in my being a well-rounded person. Countless hours were spent, after his docket ended, talking about cases that were before him and upcoming hearings. He also reinforced the fact that not only was it an awesome privilege to work as a lawyer, but it came with a lot of responsibility. The judge stressed the importance of professional civility both inside and outside the courtroom.

I soaked up all of his advice and shared with him my goals and aspirations as a lawyer. The judge was very supportive and encouraged me to consider a career as a public interest attorney. As my clerkship was coming to an end, he suggested that I apply for a staff attorney position at the Maryland Legal Aid Bureau, Inc. (Legal Aid Bureau), a highly regarded public interest law firm.

Luckily for me, shortly after my judicial clerkship ended, the Legal Aid Bureau was seeking a family law attorney in their Domestic Law Unit. The more I learned about the work the position entailed, the more I became really excited because it was exactly what I wanted to do. Also, I could not think of a better way to make a difference in the lives of the most vulnerable population of society—the poor.

The only problem was the low salary that the job paid. I had a sizable student loan debt that I placed on deferment because I felt I could not afford the monthly payments. However, I had to remind myself why I left

Corporate America and made a career change. I took a leap of faith and accepted the staff attorney position with the Legal Aid Bureau, and decided that I would accept a low salary if it meant enjoying the work that I do. I have no regrets about my decision.

To my surprise, what I found was that I was not only able to make do on a staff attorney salary of a public interest lawyer, but I was able to achieve many of my financial goals. I have been working for the Legal Aid Bureau for approximately ten years, and during that time, I've managed to

1. get my student loan out of deferment and make regular monthly payments;
2. establish and build an emergency reserve account;
3. contribute at least 15 percent of my gross income to a retirement plan;
4. buy a home on my own and make extra payments toward the mortgage principal balance each year;
5. pay off all my credit card debts;
6. travel the world and stay at high-end luxury hotels;
7. dine out and enjoy local entertainment whenever I want;
8. shop for clothes at my favorite designer stores;
9. indulge in regular pampering consisting of manicures, pedicures, and beauty salon visits; and
10. give, consistently, to causes that are important to me.

I have done all of this, while keeping my daily living expenses within my monthly take-home pay, on a public interest attorney salary. Yes, I said it—ALL ON A PUBLIC INTEREST ATTORNEY SALARY! I would also add that I am single and do not have the benefit of a spouse's income to supplement my lifestyle—nor do I have a roommate. In addition, I have never won the lottery or received an inheritance.

A lot of talented lawyers and law students do not even consider a career in public interest law because of the low salary. I often hear "I can't afford it" or "I won't be able to provide for my basic needs, let alone small luxuries." But my personal experience shows that is not true. It really comes down to how you maximize your salary in order to get the most bang for your buck. That is why I decided to write this book. I want to show how I managed my money to prove that you can not only survive but thrive on a public interest attorney salary.

I am living proof that you can live in a manner where you do not feel that you have to deprive yourself. As I write the introduction to this book, I am lying on the beach at the RIU Hotel & Resort in sunny Negril, Jamaica. This trip, I'm proud to say, had already been paid for prior to my arrival. (Yup, I paid for it all by myself on my public interest salary!) If you check out their Web site and view how phenomenally gorgeous the resort is (they did not pay me to say this), you will see that I am by no means a lady who believes in deprivation.

By writing this book, what I hope to accomplish is to get sharp lawyers and law students to seriously consider legal services organizations and not-for-profit law firms when job hunting. The fact that you are reading this book demonstrates that you are considering a career as a public interest attorney and want to know how you can live comfortably on a modest salary. Additionally, I want to encourage those who already work at public interest organizations but are contemplating leaving due to the low pay to stay by showing how you can live well as a public interest lawyer. Finally, I hope to attract those who are not fulfilled in their work at private law firms and are seeking to redirect their legal careers to help those of limited means by explaining how I managed my money.

This book is a step-by-step guide to help you flourish financially as a public interest attorney by sharing the money skills I've learned and implemented in my personal finances. The techniques that worked for me can help you create both a professionally and financially rewarding life for yourself. You may be skeptical, believing that I am offering one of those gimmicky "get-rich-quick" schemes. On the contrary, I am here to show you how, by making practical financial choices methodically and consistently, you can be prosperous and build wealth on a public interest lawyer's salary and enjoy life in the process.

You do not need to be a financial whiz or have received a masters in business administration in order to get your financial life in order. There is nothing that I did that was complex or complicated. I am an ordinary legal aid attorney who was determined to make my money work for me, and I want to share what I did so that you too can achieve financial success.

As you read, you will see that the simple financial decisions I made when handling my money can work for anyone. Regardless of your monetary situation, you can achieve financial prosperity if you are willing to actively manage your finances. To aid you on your financial journey, I have provided an Action Plan at the end of each chapter that you can implement to keep you moving.

This book is meant to be a quick read because I know that law students and lawyers are very busy and need to cut to the chase. With that said, let's get started!

CHAPTER 1
$ $ $ $

Managing Student Loan Debt
Tackling That Five-Hundred-Pound Gorilla

I want to address the issue of student loan debt first because I know it is an albatross around most lawyers' necks. Plus, I believe that none of the strategies I will share for creating personal wealth on a public interest attorney's salary will have any impact unless I deal with this matter upfront. I know many attorneys will not even consider a career as a public interest lawyer because of their looming student loan debt.

Many law students and lawyers are saddled not only with law school loans but undergraduate student loan debt as well. When all is said and done, student loan debt for many legal professionals can well exceed the $100,000 mark. Yet I can still tell you confidently that it is possible to live a good life with a hefty debt load on the salary of a public interest attorney because I am currently doing it.

While student loan obligations can be depressing, there's no doubt that this type of debt is a good debt because you are investing in yourself. Even though I wish I did not have student loan debt, I happily pay my loan each month because it has allowed me to have a rewarding career as a lawyer. I find it quite sad and disconcerting that student loans deter talented attorneys from pursuing public interest work as a meaningful legal career.

There are many lawyers who have a passion to assist those who are less privileged and financially disadvantaged. I cannot tell you the countless numbers of lawyers whom I have met who have told me that there is no way that they could live on a legal aid lawyer's salary with their exorbitant student loan debt. I tell them that it is possible because I do it and work with many attorneys who are doing the same—and we are not panhandling.

Keeping Education Costs Down

For those reading this book who are still in law school, I highly encourage you to keep your law school debt to a minimum. Federal laws prevent student loans from being discharged in bankruptcy. Failure to repay student loan debt will place a large blemish on your credit report—greatly impacting your ability to obtain credit and other types of financing in the future, including a home mortgage loan. Additionally, any tax refunds due you can be intercepted and a substantial portion of your paychecks garnished.

My advice is, while in school, take out the smallest loan that you possibly can. If you can get a part-time gig to help with your living expenses, which is what I did when I was in law school, that would certainly be in your best interest. I worked part-time at my law school's alumni office and borrowed enough money to pay for my tuition. I also worked as a research assistant for one of my professors, which paid a portion of my tuition and provided me with a modest stipend that I used for my general living expenses. I took some classes in the summer in order to graduate law school one semester early.

Despite my efforts to contain my educational costs, I still graduated law school with a substantial amount of student loan debt. (Syracuse University College of Law was certainly not cheap!) For those of you who are not totally against sharing your personal living space with someone, you may want to consider getting a reliable roommate. Splitting your expenses with someone who is responsible goes a long way in reducing your overall expenses while in law school.

Handling Current Educational Debt

If you have already graduated from law school or are about to graduate and you have significant student loan debt, do not be disheartened. You can still conquer your debt and make your monthly student loan payments manageable. Fortunately, there are many student loan repayment options offered by lenders that are tailored to accommodate a wide salary range—including that of a public interest lawyer's salary.

One thing that I would encourage you to do is to begin paying your student loan debt as quickly as possible. When you graduate from law school, you are given a six-month grace period before you are required to start making payments. However, I advise you to begin paying on your student loan during the grace period if possible. The reason is that it allows you to promptly face the music and not to conveniently "forget" that you have a student loan debt.

If I could turn back the hands of time, one thing that I would have done differently was pay my student loans immediately. I would have saved myself thousands of dollars in accrued interest if I paid *something* consistently to my lender. Additionally, it would probably have made me reconsider other purchases that I thought were "necessary" if I were already factoring my student loan debt payments as I was spending my money.

It is interesting how fast the six-month grace period goes by, and you start receiving the notices from your lender that it is time to start making your monthly payments. Most often, that is when you feel it is much easier to stick your head in the sand and pretend that you have no student loan debt by placing your student loan in either deferment or forbearance (I'll explain that later). I strongly advise against doing that unless you do not have a job or income from which to begin repaying your debt. The interest that accrues will compound the principal loan balance. Once I addressed my student loan debt (I'll soon discuss what I did), a tremendous burden was lifted off my shoulders, and I was able to focus on my ultimate dream—becoming a homeowner.

Understanding Student Loans

Most students obtain Stafford Loans, which is a type of federal loan. Federal student loans are guaranteed by the government. If you default on a federal loan, then the government will reimburse the lender and come after you for repayment of the debt. These types of loans can be subsidized, which means that the federal government is paying the interest on the loan that you have taken while you are in school. If you have your loan deferred, the government will pay the interest during deferment.

A Stafford Loan can also be unsubsidized where you, the borrower, are responsible for paying the interest that accrues. Subsidized loans are based on need, but unsubsidized loans are not. Most students (I was one of them) typically have the lender add the interest payments to an unsubsidized loan while in school because they cannot afford to pay the interest while attending school. I had both subsidized and unsubsidized federal loans in law school.

There are also private student loans, which are loans made by banks. If you default on this loan, instead of the government chasing you down for repayment, the bank or financial institution will seek you out. Private loans are not subsidized. You need to be careful with private loans as they do not offer the same type of loan repayment options as federal loans. For instance, private lenders usually do not offer loan forgiveness or the most favorable loan repayment options.

Facing the Music

As stated earlier, once you graduate, you have six months until your first student loan payment is due. Many students (again, I was one of them) do not want to face the debt primarily because this is when you realize how much debt you owe. Student loan debt will not go away, and you certainly do not want to default on your student loans.

I will note, however, that there are some circumstances where you may be able to cancel your student loan, such as in the event of your death (which won't do you much good) or if you suffer a total and permanent disability, among others. However, detailed documentation of your complete inability to work must be provided before a lender would even consider terminating your loan. Let's just face it; if you have student loan debt, you can be quite certain that you will be expected to pay it back.

If your student loan monthly payments exceed your ability to pay, then you need to contact and speak with your lender. As I stated earlier, you cannot get your student loan debt discharged in bankruptcy, and you do not want to default on your student loan. If you do default, your wages can be attached, any tax refunds due you will be intercepted, and your credit score damaged. I am not saying this to scare you, but I have seen too many people ignore their student loan debt and suffer terrible consequences down the road.

Loan Repayment Options

The good news is that there are many different ways and options to repay your student loan debt, which will enable you to live comfortably on a public interest attorney's salary. Lenders do recognize that not everyone who graduates from school—especially law school—receives a high-paying job. So do not be afraid to let them know about your financial situation. Believe it or not, lenders really do want to work with you. Student loan creditors will allow you to avail yourself of a variety of repayment plans in order to manage your debt. Some of your options are as follows:

Standard repayment. This option allows you to pay off your student loan in ten years.

Extended repayment. Under this plan, you can pay off your student loan over a period of up to twenty-five years.

Graduated repayment. This is where payments start out small, typically by paying only the loan interest, and then during the course of the loan repayment, the amount increases.

Income percentage repayment plans. If your income is low, your loan repayment is attached to a percentage of your income. Anytime your income increases, the amount of your repayment will increase (and I want you to know that your pay can increase as a public interest attorney) in accordance with the percentage applied to your income. Conversely, if your salary falls, so will your monthly payments.

Income-contingent repayment. For those who have loans backed by the federal government, with the income-contingent repayment plan, if payments are made for twenty-five years, the federal government forgives the remaining principal and interest.

Income-based repayment. For public interest attorneys and certain public service workers, Congress created an income-based repayment program under the College Cost Reduction and Access Act of 2007, which caps student loan payments at 15 percent of discretionary income for borrowers who have federally guaranteed student loans. The income-based repayment option is similar to the income-contingent repayment with forgiveness of federal student loans after twenty-five years. Student loan payments under the income-based repayment plan are typically lower than the income-contingent repayment plan. This new payment option goes into effect on July 1, 2009. For more information on income-based repayment, visit *www.ibrinfo.org*.

Deferment. This option allows you to delay your payments until a future date. It only applies to those who have federal student loans, and it can be granted for reasons such as unemployment, disability, or the continuation of your education. Interest may or may not accrue depending on whether your student loan is subsidized or unsubsidized. Please note that you are still able to make payments toward your student loans even while it is under deferment. The maximum length of your deferment will depend on your situation.

Forbearance. If you choose to forbear your student loans, you do not have to pay them for a certain period of time, but interest will accrue during the forbearance period regardless of whether the loan is subsidized or unsubsidized. Private lenders, as well as federal lenders, have this option for borrowers. Just like loan repayment deferment, you can still make payments to your student loan while in forbearance.

While it is easier to obtain a forbearance as opposed to a deferment, you still must meet certain lender requirements in order to obtain a forbearance. Similar to a deferment, the amount of time that you can forbear your loan will depend on your specific situation.

Loan consolidation. This provides those who have multiple student loans with the ability to combine them into one payment. Depending on the length of your repayment time, a consolidation could significantly lower your monthly payment because you can reduce your individual monthly loan payments by extending the life of the loan and having your payments spread out over a longer period.

As I previously mentioned, the length of a student loan is ten years, but it can be extended. If you increase the life of your loan, your monthly loan payments will be lower. However, you certainly will pay more in interest over the life of the loan. So when choosing to alter the standard ten-year repayment term, make sure that you choose wisely and carefully.

Identifying and Selecting the Best Repayment Option

When selecting a repayment option, the key is to determine the type of repayment plan that works for you. You want to make sure that your loan payment allows you the type of flexibility you need to achieve your life's goals and passions. Only you, based upon your current financial circumstances, will know what is important.

A really good online student loan calculator that you should use to help decide the best option for your circumstances can be found on FinAid, which provides information on student aid. Their Web site is *www.finaid.org/calculators*. Also, the National Consumer Law Center has created a Web site dedicated to borrowers who have student loan debt, which can be found at *www.studentloanborrowerassistance.org*.

You need to be careful on how you consolidate your loans—especially if you have both private and federal loans. Federal consolidation loans will not allow you to consolidate your private loans. In order to consolidate your private loans, you have to contact a private lender. Private lenders will allow you to consolidate your federal loans with your private loans, but I do not recommend you do that because you could lose many of the benefits that federal loans offer to borrowers in terms of interest rates, deferment and forbearance options, and repayment time lengths. Please be mindful that most loans made after July 1, 2006, have a fixed 6.8 percent interest rate. Therefore, loan consolidation may not get you a better rate. Also, with some exceptions, you can only consolidate your student loans one time. If you choose to consolidate your student loans, then it is important to shop around in order to get the best rate.

If after crunching the numbers, exploring loan consolidations, and investigating various repayment options, you still find yourself unable to come up with a payment that is affordable, you are not out of luck. You can negotiate your own monthly payment. Most people don't know this (I surely didn't).

In order to do this, you must provide a detailed explanation stating why you need a more affordable monthly payment. This is where you let the lender know, in writing, your unique financial situation. You will have to provide proof of your income (or lack thereof), along with an itemized list of all your bills and expenses.

If you have a federal loan, contact the U.S. Department of Education and complete a Statement of Financial Status. If your loan is through a private lender, then you must contact the lender directly. As I stated earlier, you would be surprised how lenders are willing to work with you. The important thing is to get into the habit of paying something toward your student loan. That way you don't conveniently "forget" about it. As the saying goes, "Out of sight, out of mind."

Handling My Student Loans

When the six-month grace period of my student loan ended, I took advantage of both the deferment and forbearance options. Even though I now wish I hadn't, at the time, I felt that was what I needed to do in order to stay afloat. However, even during those periods, I occasionally made nominal student loan payments because I did not want to completely ignore the fact that I had the debt.

I decided to tackle my student loan debt head-on when I made the decision to become a homeowner. The first thing I did was to consolidate all of my loans so that I only needed to make one monthly payment. By consolidating my student loans, I was able to lock it in at a low interest rate.

Interest rates for student loans are low compared to other types of loans. As a result of the consolidation, I was able to slice my interest rate of 8.24 percent practically in half to the tune of 4.65 percent. With advances in technology, many bills can now be paid from your bank account. Student loans are no different. Lenders may reduce your interest rate if you agree to have your student loan payments automatically taken from your bank account. I selected that option and was able to shave a quarter of a percentage point off my interest rate.

My lender allowed me to choose the date that I would have my student loan deducted from my bank account. I chose the twenty-eighth of each month because I got paid biweekly, and I wanted to make sure that my loan payments were deducted from my second paycheck each month. Since my paychecks were directly deposited into my checking account, I was very confident that I would have sufficient funds in my checking account at all times to pay my student loan debt without incurring an insufficient funds charge on my account.

Psychologically, I like paying my loan debt this way because I hardly think about my student loan debt anymore. Before I consolidated my student loans, each time I received my bill, opening the loan statements would make my stomach churn. During the times when I decided to pay something toward my student loan, I would get very depressed and would feel disheartened because it was like the debt was always in my face.

I did not want to pretend that the loan no longer existed because it allowed me to obtain my law school education at Syracuse University, and I'm doing work that I absolutely love. However, I still did not want it glaring at me. Now that I have the student debt payments automatically taken from my checking account, I only have to think about it when I reconcile my checkbook.

Additionally, your student loan interest rate can decrease even more if you pay your student loan payments on time for forty-eight months. For me, that was even more of an incentive to get my payments deducted directly from my bank account. Since I took advantage of the automatic payment and timed it so that my payments would be withdrawn by my lender after my second paycheck of the month, my student loan payments were always paid on time. The key is to make sure that you have sufficient funds in your account to cover the payment when it comes due.

After the forty-eight months of on-time loan payments were completed, my lender reduced my student loan interest rate by one full percentage point. So I went from having an original student loan interest rate of 8.24 percent to a current interest rate of 3.65 percent—all by addressing my student loan debt by taking them out of deferment and forbearance (now you can see why I regret not doing this earlier).

I decided to select a twenty-five-year repayment term for my student loan because that would reduce my overall monthly payments and make them more manageable. I'll admit, I had a lot of anxiety about selecting such a long repayment term. However, I knew by doing this that I could comfortably make payments on my meager salary and still have money left over to pursue my goals which were traveling the world, becoming a homeowner, and eliminating credit card debt, to name a few (I will address values and financial goals in the next chapter).

I knew that when I looked back on my life, I wanted to think about all the things that I did to make my life pleasurable and full of meaning. I certainly knew that I would not be lamenting over my student loan debt. So I was able to put things in a proper perspective and live with my decision to extend my repayment term.

That, however, does not mean that I will not try to pay off my student loan earlier. My plan is to make extra payments toward the principal whenever I can in order to reduce the amount that I will ultimately pay in interest and shave a couple of years off the length of the repayment term. Also, I knew that I could knock out more of the loan principal by making extra payments because I had already gotten my interest rate reduced.

All of my student loans were federal loans serviced by Citibank Student Loan Corporation. I decided to consolidate all of my debts with them because they offered a very low interest rate. It is important to shop around for lenders with whom you can consolidate your student loans for the most competitive interest rate.

Contacting Lenders

If you have loans with various lenders, you will need to contact different banks in order to consolidate. Although I did not use Sallie Mae, this would be a good starting place to determine the best way to consolidate your debt. You can contact Sallie Mae at 1-888-2-Sallie (1-888-272-5543) or by visiting their Web site at *www.salliemae.com*. I would also recommend calling the U.S. Department of Education at 1-800-557-7392 or visiting their Web site at *http://loanconsolidation.ed.gov* to learn more about student loan consolidations. If you have private loans, call your lender(s) and find out if they offer any debt consolidation programs.

Financial Incentives

Uncle Sam also will allow you to deduct a portion of the student loan interest that you have paid from your taxes. There are, however, income limitations on the deductions. It is important that you check with a tax preparer to see if you are eligible. In the past, I have been able to take advantage of these tax breaks—which ultimately led to more money in my pocket in the form of tax refunds.

Loan Forgiveness and Repayment Assistance Programs

One thing that is definitely worth considering, if you are eligible, are loan forgiveness programs. Depending on where you live, are employed, attended school, and the type of work that you do, loan forgiveness may be an option for you. There are new programs offered to forgive student loans taken directly from the federal government (also called direct loans) for borrowers working in public service.

Beginning October 1, 2007, under the College Cost Reduction and Access Act of 2007, public interest attorneys (and other public service workers) who have paid their qualifying federal student loans on time for ten years while working at a public interest organization will have the remaining balance on their student loans forgiven by the federal government. Recognizing the need for good lawyers to represent poor people, there are many organizations, schools, and foundations that will pay some, if not all, of your student loan debt.

Recently, my employer, the Legal Aid Bureau, has been hiring students from the University of Baltimore School of Law who will have their third year of law school student loan debt forgiven if they work for a minimum of three years as a public interest attorney at our firm. More and more schools are offering such programs, and I think this is wonderful because it certainly helps to ease the burden of student loan debt for those interested in working as public interest attorneys. Also, it reduces the amount of job turnover at legal services organizations.

In the State of Maryland, the Maryland Higher Education Commission sponsors the Janet L. Hoffman Loan Repayment Assistance Program. This program provides grants toward the repayment of student loan debt. A few years ago, I received $5,000 from them to apply toward my student loan. This, in combination with the reduced student loan interest rate that I procured, was an ego boost for me and served as great encouragement that I really can conquer my student loan debt.

Out of curiosity, I wanted to see if there were other states offering student loan forgiveness programs. I went on the Internet and googled *Student Loan Forgiveness Programs* just to see what was available. It appears that throughout the country, there are quite a few loan forgiveness and repayment programs out there. But it certainly is not enough to address the number of lawyers and law students who are interested in working in the public interest legal arena and seek to receive monetary assistance to reduce or eliminate their student loan debt.

A Web site that provides valuable information on law schools and states that have repayment assistance and forgiveness programs is from an organization called Equal Justice Works. Equal Justice Works (previously known as the National Association for Public Interest Law) is a not-for-profit organization that provides training and support for lawyers and law students who desire to serve the low-income population with their legal difficulties and challenges. Equal Justice Works creates opportunities for lawyers and law students to work in the public interest field. They are located at 2120 L Street, Northwest, Suite 450, Washington, DC 20037-1541 and can be reached at (202) 466-3686. Check out their Web site at *www.equaljusticeworks.org* for more information.

When I browsed their Web site, I found that it supplied a wealth of information and, most of all, provided links to the various state Loan Repayment Assistance Programs (LRAP) throughout the country. Realizing the work that must be done in this area, it also provides information on how to create a statewide LRAP. Additionally, the American Bar Association has a Web site dedicated to detailing information about state LRAPs. You can review it at *www.abanet.org/legalservices/lrap/state/stateprograms.html*.

Summing It All Up

For most of us, student loans are a fact of life, and it pretty much does not go away until it is paid off. But it does not have to be the obstacle that prevents you from working as a public interest attorney. What it requires is for you to acknowledge your student loan debt, select a repayment option, and begin making payments as soon as possible.

Start with small monthly payments, preferably no more than 15 percent of your monthly take-home pay. As your income permits, try to increase your payments or make extra payments periodically. Before you know it, your student loan debt will be a thing of the past.

> ## Action Plan
>
> 1. Contact your student loan provider to discuss repayment options and lower interest rates.
>
> 2. Choose or negotiate a repayment option where your loan payments do not exceed more than 15 percent of your monthly take-home pay.
>
> 3. Have your loan payments automatically deducted from your bank account.
>
> 4. When you find yourself able to make an extra payment, write a note to the lender and specifically state on the check that the payment is to be applied toward the principal balance.

CHAPTER 2

Identifying Values And Creating Financial Goals
Deciding What Matters Most

Regardless of the amount of money you make, money will slip through your fingers unless you know what you want to achieve with the money you earn. The way to properly manage your money and make it work for you is to set financial goals. How you define your goals and succeed in achieving them is by identifying your values.

The way to determine your values is to ask yourself: "What matters most to me?" Take a moment and think about how your life would be if money was no longer an issue. Visualize what makes you happy and satisfied. Forget about your bills and debts just for a moment and ask yourself: "If I could do anything in the world, what would I be doing?" Write what comes to your mind. Don't censor yourself. The thoughts that you have written will give you great insight on what your values are.

Still having a hard time spotting your core values? OK, let me help. Imagine that you won the $250,000,000 mega lottery (hey, it can happen), and now money is no longer an issue. What would you be doing with your time and your money? Would you spend more time with your family and friends? Maybe you would volunteer at a local Boys & Girls Club. How about traveling the world? Maybe you would donate money to Habitat for Humanity. Your responses will reflect what your values are.

Say for instance, you decided that you were going to give some of the lottery money to support a worthy cause; a value that can be identified as being important to you is generosity. If you decided that you would spend more time with family and friends if you were a multimillionaire, then relationships would be considered of significant value to you.

Other examples of core values are excellence, self-sufficiency, leadership, productivity, honesty, patience, and education. The possibilities of determining what is important to you are endless. Taking the time to define your values not only improves your financial life but other aspects of your life as well.

As a public interest attorney, I often hear my colleagues talk about needing to make more money and never having enough money. The common thread expressed is the desire of not wanting to live paycheck to paycheck. This phenomenon is not unique to my coworkers. I have heard people in other professions who make double or triple the amount of money of a public interest attorney complain about the difficulty of being able to make ends meet. I am convinced that many of these feelings of frustration can be eliminated if people got in touch with their values and set financial goals based on those values.

Being Honest

When identifying your values, you need to get real. Your values need to be just that—yours. You must own them. Do not judge the merits of your values based upon what others think or believe should be your values.

Even if you are in a committed relationship or have a family, you still are an individual with your own views, thoughts, and perspectives on life. If you have a family, you certainly can establish what values are important to your family. However, that is not a pass to neglect assessing your own personal values and establishing individual goals.

Creating Financial Goals

Once you have identified your values, you then need to create financial goals based upon those values. It is crucial that you write your goals down regardless of what they are. Even if you believe your goals are outrageous, write them down anyway. You just may surprise yourself and find that they are achievable. Also, your financial goals should be specific. Instead of saying that you want to save money for emergencies, write down exactly how much you want to save and where you are going to save that money. For example, you can write, "I will save $1,500 for emergencies in a credit union savings account." Instead of saying you want to start saving for retirement, you can be more specific by writing, "I will direct 5 percent of my gross income into an individual retirement account."

Types of Financial Goals

Financial goals are typically divided into three types: short-term, intermediate-term, and long-term. As a rule of thumb, short-term goals are goals that would take less than five years to reach. Intermediate-term goals are those that can be reached within five to ten years. Finally, long-term goals are anything that you want to accomplish in ten years or more. Make sure you set a deadline to achieve your goals. If you find that the time frame is not realistic, you can always change it. But give yourself an end date so that you have something specific to look forward to.

My suggestion is that when you set goals, make sure that at least one of your goals is short-term. Psychologically, I believe it is important to experience quick results so that you will not give up on your longer-term goals. When you see your goals being achieved, you are motivated; and most important, you feel a sense of fulfillment.

Do not write your goals down and forget about them. Review them daily. I have all my goals written in my personal planner. My planner goes with me everywhere—even on vacations. Many times when I am waiting in line at the grocery store or at the doctor's office, I whip out my planner and review my goals. I find that I am less likely to act in ways that go against my goals when they are ingrained in me.

Aligning Your Goals With Your Values

When reviewing your goals, make sure that they line up with your identified values. The closer your goals are in sync with your values, the more likely you are to act in ways that will allow you to achieve those goals. You may find yourself writing and prioritizing several goals or even rethinking your values. That is perfectly fine. Many people do not take the time to sit down and focus on their goals and values, so when they begin to do this, they find it quite difficult. Please don't give up. Once your values and goals become clear, you will be able to act in a manner that serves your best interests.

I can tell you, firsthand, that when I began to focus and envision the type of life I wanted and how I could best achieve my dreams and goals on a modest public interest attorney salary, I became unstoppable. My life has not only been rich and rewarding personally and professionally but financially as well. Let me explain.

Even on a low salary, one of my core values is financial independence. Financial independence can mean different things to different people. What it meant for me was not having ongoing credit card debt, contributing at least 10 percent of my gross income to my 401(k) plan, having at least $3,000 in emergency savings, and having all of my expenses (including my student loan and mortgage payments) less than my income. I did not ever want to find myself in a position where I would have to ask people for money—not even my family.

Another value that is important to me is having fun. What I consider fun is going to the movies, out to dinner, and dancing—especially to Latin music—whenever I want. In the past, whenever friends wanted to get together to catch a dinner and a movie, I typically would not have two nickels to rub together. So either I would not participate, or if I did, I would end up charging it on my credit card. Since I wanted to have fun, I developed a financial goal, which was to have $250 in a savings account dedicated only to fun activities. So if I want to catch an evening play, I can just go. If I want to indulge myself at a fondue restaurant, no sweat; I just do it. If I want to spend a weekend in Ocean City, Maryland—I'll jump in my car and go. The result, I do not ever feel deprived. Now that is a good feeling!

A third value that is important to me is traveling and experiencing different cultures. I grew up watching the television show *Lifestyles of the Rich and Famous* and would marvel at all of the beautiful destinations celebrities would vacation. My jaw would drop in awe of the glamorous resorts and hotels that they would patronize. I always knew that I wanted to vacation like that. Based on that value, my goal is to travel overseas, in style, at least once a year.

I am very happy to say that I have not only achieved the above goals, but I have surpassed many of them. Like I stated, I currently contribute 15 percent of my gross income to my 401(k) retirement plan and have several months living expenses saved in a mutual fund account for emergencies. Additionally, I have no credit card debt—zip, zero, zilch! Whenever I use my credit cards, I can pay the balance in full. I maintain $250 in a savings account that I use solely for fun. Also, I have taken an international vacation every year—and stayed in some really fancy hotels. (I have the pictures to prove it!)

All of this was done on my salary as a public interest attorney, and it all started by writing my values and financial goals. If you still have not thought about or established your values and financial goals, I suggest that you do it right now. Studies have shown that when you write down your goals, you significantly increase your chances of obtaining them.

When you achieve your financial goals, you feel more relaxed and calm because you are in control of your money. As a result, your quality of life increases because you now have a reason to get up in the morning, and you feel a sense of accomplishment so that you sleep well at night. I am certainly living proof of that! However, it is not enough to establish your values and goals; you must move to action.

In the next few chapters, I will show you how I moved to action and achieved the financial goals that many aspire to achieve, such as owning a home, saving for retirement, and paying off credit card debt. My hope is that it will not only motivate you but help to jump-start your own financial goals so that you can achieve the type of success and fulfillment that I have experienced in managing my money as a public interest attorney.

Action Plan

1. Think about and write down the type of life you envision for yourself.

2. Identify and write down your values as a result of your vision.

3. Write down at least three financial goals based on your values and make sure that at least one of your goals is short-term.

4. Review your values and goals daily.

CHAPTER 3
$ $ $ $

Developing A Spending Plan
Moving to Action

How many times have you withdrawn money from an ATM and by the end of the day, the money is gone, and you have no clue where the money went? Countless times, right? Well, you are not alone. This is a common occurrence among many people. It would happen to me often until I developed a personal Spending Plan.

A Spending Plan is a written guide that you create to determine how you will manage your money. When you create a Spending Plan, you control and actively direct your money toward those things that are important to you. When you are conscious about how you spend your money, you prevent it from slipping between your fingers. Developing a Spending Plan is really not difficult. All you have to do is examine your needs and wants based upon your values and goals and decide how much you will spend on a particular need or want.

Tracking Your Spending

The best way to create a successful Spending Plan is to determine how you are currently spending your money on a daily basis. Grab a notepad and pen and write down everything you buy each day for the next four weeks. By doing this, you will really start to pay attention to what you are purchasing with your money. It is best to write down your purchase at the time you buy something. Sometimes, it is not always possible to do that. If you are unable to immediately write it down, make sure that you do it when you get home.

At the end of each day, add up the cost of everything that you bought. Be sure to include any checks written and any items purchased with a credit card. This will give you a good idea of what you are spending your money on. If you do this for another two months, you will get an even clearer picture on your overall spending because more than likely, expenses that occur periodically will surface, like car insurance, gifts, and professional dues to name a few.

After you have tracked your spending, compare your total expenses to the amount of income you earned for that month. If your income is more than what you spent, then you are living within your means. If not, you are clearly living above your means. Regardless of the final result, review your expenses and honestly decide which items you could have done without. To get you thinking critically about this, ask yourself if any of the purchases were in line with your values and financial goals. If they were, then ask if you could have bought them for less money elsewhere or if the purchases could have been delayed. You will take all this information to help create your own personal Spending Plan.

When tracking your daily expenditures, you do not need to be too exact. Feel free to round your purchases up or down to the nearest dollar. It will all average out in the end. If you make expense tracking onerous and burdensome, then you probably will not stick to it. After you have reviewed your expenses, highlight the ones that you determined to be nonessential and add those up. Do the same for those expenses that you considered essential. Remember, you are in the driver's seat, so you must decide what expenses are crucial. Review your financial goals and see if any of the expenditures furthered any of your financial goals. Now that you have started tracking your money, you are ready to create your own personal Spending Plan.

Begin your Spending Plan by allocating money to each of your financial goals. In other words, pay yourself first. Let me repeat: PAY YOURSELF FIRST! You may be saying, "But I have tons of credit card debt!" My response, "Pay yourself first!" You may also be thinking that after you pay your monthly bills, there is nothing left over to save. Again my response is "Pay yourself first!" It does not matter what your present financial situation is; I will never change my response, which is to PAY YOURSELF FIRST! The reason why you should pay yourself first is because it makes your desires and needs a top priority. Emotionally, you will feel empowered and confident over how you handle your money when you funnel your money toward the various goals deemed important to you.

The Price Paid For Not Tracking Your Spending

One thing I have found is that if you are not conscious about how your money is being utilized, it can easily be squandered away on things that have no meaning or value to you. I always remember saying if I made more money, I would be able to do X, Y, and Z; then I would get more money and not know where the money went. I would sing the same old song about what I would do if I made more money, only for the cycle to repeat itself. Not anymore. Any time I learned of a pending pay increase, regardless of the amount, I would actively review the areas in my Spending Plan where I could *reduce* my expenditures so that any increase in income would stay in my pocket and be funneled to achieve any of my financial goals.

Using the Spending Plan to Achieve Your Financial Goals

Start by opening up a separate savings account for each financial goal. By segregating individual bank accounts to address each goal, you can clearly see your progress in reaching them. Do not lump all of your goals into one account because it could result in an inaccurate picture of where you are with respect to your financial goals.

Let me give you an example; I have a savings account at a local credit union dedicated only to car repair expenses. I like to have a balance of $1,000 in that account at all times. I also have an Internet savings account that is only used to pay for my luxury vacations. Usually when the account reaches $1,300, I feel comfortable that I can start actively planning for my vacation.

If I were to lump these accounts together into a single bank account, I really would not be able to distinguish how much is earmarked for a vacation as opposed to the car expense. If I placed all the money for those two goals in one account, and the account balance is, for example, $1,800, I may lull myself into thinking I can pay for a luxury vacation in advance of my intended travel date. However, if I see that only $800 is in my vacation account for a trip that I want to take in less than three months, I would know that I would have to hustle and direct more money toward my vacation account in order to enjoy a guilt-free, upscale vacation. I would not have known that if I combined that money in an account with another financial goal. It is similar to purchasing a utensil divider to separate your spoons, knives, and forks. By separating each utensil, you can see how much of each you have.

It is not hard to open a new savings account. It took me less than ten minutes to open up accounts for each of my financial goals. In your Spending Plan, decide how much of your money will go to each of these accounts. If you feel really stretched for funds, start by saving 1 percent of your take-home pay.

For example, if your take-home pay is $900, then take $9 and apply it to your goals. While $9 may seem small, it is nothing to scoff at. If you save $9 biweekly, you will have $234 plus interest by the end of the year. If you save $9 per week, at the end of the year, you will have $468. Now if you got aggressive and saved $9 every other day, you will have $1,638 at the end of the year. If you really want to get super-disciplined and save $9 per day, you will have $3,285 plus interest.

It goes to show you that small savings can really add up over time. Starting small helps build momentum. Contrary to what you may believe, as you begin to save more money to fund your goals and dreams, you will find it easier to live on the money that remains because you are acting in accordance with your values. Next thing you know, you could find yourself putting 20 percent or more of your take-home pay into various financial goal accounts.

Paying Yourself First

It is important that you get into the habit of paying yourself first. Anyone who has created true wealth always paid himself first. By paying yourself first, what you are saying, in the truest sense of the word, is that you matter. People who work at legal services organizations or nonprofit companies give of themselves, both in time and lower pay, to assist others in need. I work among very bright attorneys who could easily obtain lucrative salaries at private law firms, yet they commit to providing quality legal representation to the poor. I believe the best way to acknowledge your hard work and sacrifice is to pay yourself first.

When I began to pay myself first, I started quite small by making tiny deposits into different savings accounts. I was determined not to set myself up for failure. Over time, I gradually increased my savings contributions as I became more in control of my money. I found that I did not even miss the money I set aside because I became accustomed to taking money off the top from each paycheck for my savings. As I saw myself approaching or achieving my goals, I began to look for more ways to save money.

Again, start small. If tackling all of your financial goals seems daunting, then focus only on one goal for three months. After three months, assess how you did. You may find that you want to add another goal. Soon you will find that you can increase the amount you are able to save.

If you still think you don't have any money to save, start by saving all of your change. Whenever you buy something, use only paper money. At the end of the day, put all of your change in a jar. Count up your change at the end of the month and deposit it in a savings account. This is painless and fun.

I established my fun account by saving my change. At the end of the month, I usually have at least $20 worth of change that I can deposit. As I stated earlier, my local fun savings account typically has $250 in it at all times. I use that money to go out to dinner, dessert, or catch a movie on a moment's notice without jeopardizing my monthly Spending Plan.

Sometimes, I would deposit my change into my car repair account and vacation account. It depends on what my needs and goals are at any given time. To get an even better financial footing, I recently opened up another Internet savings account to save money for periodic expenses such as my homeowner's association dues, bar association dues, and water bill. As a result, when these periodic bills come due, my Spending Plan does not go down the drain. Also, I sometimes save my change and direct it toward my emergency savings. By doing this, I can handle any unplanned emergency and am less reliant on my credit cards to bail me out of a jam.

If you participate in your employer's retirement plan, you are really paying yourself first—even before Uncle Sam gets his cut of your earnings. It does not get any better than that. If you were to invest a portion of your income in an employer-sponsored retirement plan, you are taxed on your gross income less the amount that you contributed to your retirement plan. The reason is that the government wants to give you an incentive to start your own savings for retirement. While there are limits to the amount you can contribute each year, the financial limits really affect higher wage earners. (I'll be discussing retirement investing in the next chapter.)

Hopefully, I have convinced you that even despite having a low salary, you can save some of your money. After you decide how much you will save toward your various goals, allocate how much you will spend on your essential needs. Essential items are those things needed in order to survive. It usually consists of your rent or mortgage, utilities, food, etc. Look at what is left and allocate the rest to all the nonessential items, like gifts, cable, magazine subscriptions, etc. You are in excellent shape if you have enough money to meet your savings goals, essential needs, and nonessential wants. But do not be dismayed if you come up short. I want you to keep working on your Spending Plan until what you spend equals what you earn.

I had to rewrite my Spending Plan at least a dozen times before the numbers added up. Keep in mind that you are in charge when designing your Spending Plan. Here are general guidelines that I follow when determining the percentage of my salary that I will allocate to each spending category.

Janine's Spending Plan

Spending Category	Percentage of Money Allocated
Savings Goals	17%
Housing (including utilities)	35%
Food	6%
Clothing	4%
Auto	9%
Entertainment	4%
Gifts	3%
Personal Grooming	4%
Charitable Giving	7%
Student Loan Debt	8%
Miscellaneous	3%

Now remember, this is my Spending Plan, and I have been doing this for several years. I was not always saving 17 percent of my income. When I began my Spending Plan, most of my money went toward paying my credit card debt. Therefore, your Spending Plan may be completely different from my own. The only thing that I ask you to do when creating your Spending Plan is to pay yourself first.

I am always looking for ways to save money. Here are some ideas and suggestions that can help you save money:

1. Save on gas by combining all your errands into one
2. Wash your car yourself
3. Raise your deductible on your car insurance
4. Carpool to work
5. Use public transportation at least once a week
6. If you live close enough to your job, walk
7. Save on dry cleaning by using an at-home dry cleaning product
8. Brown-bag your lunch to work (trust me, this is a BIG money saver)
9. Instead of dining out with friends, have a potluck
10. Reduce the number of times you eat out each month
11. Cook your own gourmet meals (I love Rachael Ray's *30 Minute Meals* cookbooks)
12. Buy generic brands at the supermarket
13. Buy nonperishable items in bulk
14. Use coupons (only if you plan on buying a particular item)
15. Rent movies
16. Instead of buying or renting DVDs, swap with a friend, neighbor, or family member
17. If you must go to the movie theatre, see a matinee show
18. Skip the popcorn and soda at the movies and eat beforehand
19. Buy clothes that are classic and not easily "dated"
20. Buy clothes only when they are on sale

21. Shop at outlet malls or consignment shops
22. Lower your thermostat in the winter and use blankets to stay warm
23. Turn off the air conditioner when you are not home
24. Only use your dishwasher or laundry machine when you have a full load
25. Borrow books from the library instead of purchasing them
26. Cancel your magazine subscriptions and read them at the library (though I refuse to cancel my *O, The Oprah Magazine* subscription)
27. Extend the time between hair and other personal grooming appointments
28. Shop online for deals before going to the store
29. Cut out the premium cable channels and just get basic cable
30. Cancel your cable television
31. Lower your cell phone service by one plan
32. Get rid of your landline and just use your cell phone
33. Withdraw money from your bank's ATM to avoid bank fees
34. When using your debit card, use it as a credit card to avoid debit fees
35. Pay your bills online to save costs on postage
36. If you own a home and car, use the same insurance company to receive a discount

Try some of these ideas (I use many of them) to help you live within your means. For other approaches to saving money and reducing spending, view *www.stretcher.com*. You do not have to apply all these saving methods all of the time; but if you would do some of them most of the time, you can save more money to allocate toward your financial goals. When you begin to reach your goals, some things that you used to spend your hard-earned money on may no longer be as important. When you pay yourself first, you find that you do not even miss the money. If you do find yourself repeatedly in a jam and are in need of money, look at other areas in your Spending Plan where you can cut back. If you are putting an unrealistic amount of money aside into savings, consider reducing the amount of money contributed but don't stop saving toward your goals. Having something specific that you can look forward to each day keeps you enthused and motivated—which increases the quality of your life.

Reviewing Your Spending Plan

It is not enough to create a Spending Plan and not refer to it often. When I first outlined my Spending Plan, I would not look at it until the end of the month. When I did, I would always overspend on most, if not all, of my spending categories. I would vow to do better the next month only to blow my Spending Plan again.

In order to monitor how my daily spending was measuring up to my monthly Spending Plan, I would conduct a weekly spending review. On the seventh, fourteenth, twenty-first, and twenty-eighth day of each month, I would review my spending in each of my assigned categories to check if I was staying within my Spending Plan. For example, my monthly gas limit is $250. On the seventh of the month, I would review my expenditure list for the week and see how much I spent on gas. Let's say during the first week of the month, I spent $50 on gas, I would write it down on a piece of paper. Now on the fourteenth day of the month, I would review my daily expense list from day 8 to day 14 of the month. If I spent $65 on gas during that week, I'll indicate that I spent a total of $115.00 ($50 [week 1] + $65 [week 2]) during the first two weeks of the month. On day 21, if I bought more gas, I would add it to the total from the previous weeks. If, say for example, on the twenty-first of the month, I realized that I spent a total of $200 during the month, then I will know that I can only spend $50 on gas for the rest of the month in order to stay within my Spending Plan. Depending how close I come to my limit, I may reassess how much driving I really need to do. If I went over my gas allocation, I would have to take that money from another spending category (not my savings).

I followed this similar approach with my other spending categories and found that I was becoming more and more conscious of how I was handling my money. As a result, I began to stay within my Spending Plan each month. Sometimes I would still find myself overspending on a particular spending category (typically clothes), but I would not beat myself up about it. All I would do is scrutinize and take a hard look at my expenditure list to see if there were any items purchased that were frivolous and unnecessary. I would whip out my values and goals list to help keep me honest. If I found myself repeatedly overspending in a category that was important to me, I would adjust my Spending Plan by allocating more money to the category where I was consistently overspending and reduce my spending in another category. By using my Spending Plan to reach my financial goals, I am thriving not only financially but in all other aspects of my life as well.

Handling "Extra" Money

Another way to help you live within your means is to direct any unexpected money or windfall toward your financial goals. For instance, when you get paid biweekly, there are two months each year when you get three paychecks. My colleagues and I call it the "extra check." I love the "extra check" months because I use that money to further my financial goals and to get me back on track in the event I strayed from my Spending Plan.

I will typically keep a portion of the "extra check" money in my checking account in order to ease the squeeze during those times I run low on cash. I spread the remaining money toward my financial goals. When I was saddled with credit card debt, I used that money to pay down the debt that I owed. I also used some of that money to pay extra on my mortgage. I would also use that money to treat myself to a nice massage or spa pedicure and new outfit.

I sometimes have to travel for work, and I get reimbursed for mileage and parking. When I complete the travel reimbursement form, I decide how I will use the money when I am reimbursed. Recently, I purchased a stainless steel refrigerator, which provided a $65 rebate. I decided, in advance, how I would use the rebate check once I received it. I just don't blindly absorb that money into my daily expenses because if I did, I can guarantee you that the money will not be deposited into any of my financial goal accounts.

When you do your own weekly spending review, take that time to review the progress you are making on your different financial goal accounts. I get very excited every time I see my savings account balances increase. Knowing that I am quickly approaching my goals gives me even more incentive to spend within my Spending Plan because that will enable me to funnel more money into my goal accounts in order to realize my dreams.

Even with a modest salary, you too can live within your means and thrive. There is no reason for you to have to live paycheck to paycheck. You deserve to use some of your money for your personal enjoyment. All it takes is having a reasonable monthly Spending Plan, tracking your expenses daily, and reviewing your spending list every week. Try it and you will see what I mean.

Action Plan

1. Track your spending for at least thirty days.

2. Create your own Spending Plan and make sure you include saving toward your financial goals in your plan.

3. Open a savings or investment account for each of your financial goals.

4. Place money each pay period into the savings and investment accounts that you have established.

5. Compare your spending tracking list every seven days to your Spending Plan.

6. Make adjustments to your Spending Plan if necessary.

CHAPTER 4
$ $ $ $

Saving For Retirement
Securing Your Financial Future

It is easy when you are receiving a modest salary as a public interest attorney to put off a long-term savings strategy such as investing in a retirement plan. Let's face it, you are trying to make ends meet on a daily basis, so it becomes relatively easy to delay saving for retirement. The rationale usually goes something like this: "Once I'm able to get a 'handle' on my finances, then I'll start saving for retirement." But then life happens; the car breaks down, a child gets sick, rent or property taxes increase—the list goes on and on. As a result, you never end up getting around to it.

Excuses For Not Investing

Some people, especially those in their twenties and thirties, don't believe they need to start thinking about investing for retirement because it won't be happening any time soon. Well, I am here to tell you that is precisely why you should start investing in your own retirement because the longer you regularly save for retirement, the more money you will have when it comes time to retire. Also, you won't have to invest as much each month because you have time on your side.

Another excuse given for why one cannot start saving for retirement is that investing is only for the rich. Well, let me clue you in on something: there are people who have six-figure salaries who do not believe they make enough money to save for their retirement (go figure). It doesn't require a lot of money to invest in a retirement plan. You can contribute as little as $20 per month and end up with a sizeable nest egg by the time you retire.

Usually, when most people actually begin thinking about retirement, it is because they find themselves near retirement age and realize that they have little to nothing saved. I did not want that to happen to me, and I certainly don't want that to happen to you. This is why I am urging you, regardless of your age and your income, to begin saving for retirement NOW! You will not regret it. I attend many free financial seminars and notice that I am typically one of the youngest people in the audience. Many people who attend are approaching or are at retirement age, and I always hear someone say that they wish that they started investing in a retirement plan earlier.

I know some people find any kind of investing too difficult and risky. I learned the basics of investing by reading numerous personal finance books and magazines. As I read, I realized that retirement investing was not so difficult after all. While there are hundreds of investment products out there, you can pick and choose funds based upon your retirement goals and your tolerance for risk. Since I was in my late twenties when I started investing for retirement, I knew I could handle significant risk because I had several decades ahead of me before I would retire. The stock market, I saw, had an overall history of an upward trajectory, despite daily fluctuations in the market. Therefore, I knew if I invested regularly and consistently, I would prevail and make money over the long term.

Perils of Not Investing

If you are afraid to risk losing your money by investing, you should know that by not investing, you actually are losing money because of inflation. Inflation is what causes the cost of buying things to increase. What you pay for things now will be much higher five, ten, and thirty years from now. By investing, you increase the chances of having your money grow over time so that it either keeps up with or beats inflation. Think about how much you paid for gas ten years ago to fill up your car. Regardless of where you live, you are certainly paying more for gas now. My point is that you are not avoiding risk by not investing in a retirement plan.

In the chapter about student loan debt, I lamented over the fact that I did not deal with my student loan debt earlier. Fortunately, that was not the case when it came to retirement investing. When I first started working at the Legal Aid Bureau, I became very interested in personal finance and investing because I really wanted to make my money work for me. One of my values is to engage in the type of work that would make me feel fulfilled. My work at Legal Aid was doing just that, and I did not want to forgo the satisfaction I felt due to lack of money. I've always heard it said that it is not about how much money you make but how much of it you keep. I learned that saving for retirement was one of the best ways to keep Uncle Sam out of my wallet.

Some organizations and companies offer pension benefits to their employees. My employer is one of them. Just note that employers offering these kinds of benefits are becoming a thing of the past, and it is unlikely that the amount received from a pension will be enough to live on comfortably. Many who will receive a pension and have convinced themselves that they can't save for retirement will probably make their retirement savings strategy their pension and social security. It is unlikely that these payments combined will cover what will be needed to live on in retirement.

While I do not believe that social security will go belly-up, I certainly know that it will not provide for my needs and wants once I retire. Any money received from social security or a pension should be to supplement your own retirement savings. Depending on social security as your sole source of retirement income is not a smart decision. Don't use your company pension plan (if they are offering one) or the receipt of social security as an excuse for not implementing your own retirement savings. Those who do could wind up in their retirement years with a lower standard of living.

Retirement Plans

Employer-sponsored retirement plans are commonly known as 401(k) plans. Depending on the type of company you work for, they can also be called 403(b) plans. Both plans operate in a similar manner by allowing employees to contribute money from each paycheck for their own retirement.

Any money you contribute to your employer-sponsored retirement account is yours, not your employer's. Your employer may contribute to your retirement plan by way of a match. Usually the employer requires an employee to work for them for a specific number of years before any rights to the money that they matched can be accessed. Other than that, your contributions to your retirement belong to you, and you can take it with you when you leave your employer.

When I first began learning about investing, the Legal Aid Bureau did not offer a 401(k) plan to their employees. Shortly after I had been working there, they offered a 401(k) through the American Bar Association. I remember clearly when the plan representative came to my office to make a presentation. Fortunately, I had already researched retirement savings and was able to follow and understand the presenter. At the conclusion of the seminar, there was no hesitation on my part to officially begin my retirement savings.

Before I tell you how I went about investing in my employer's 401(k) plan, I want to give you a general overview of the various types of investments. I want to state first that I am not a professional investment advisor (remember, I am a public interest attorney), but I have been investing in my 401(k) retirement, on my own, for more than nine years. So feel free to get professional financial help if that would make you more comfortable with investing.

Finding and Selecting a Financial Planner

If you decide to seek the assistance of a financial planner, get referrals from family, friends, and colleagues. Make sure you interview several before choosing one. Ask about their educational background and whether they hold any accreditations or professional licenses. Additionally, you want to know whether they charge their clients a flat fee or are compensated by commissions for their services (flat fees are the best, commissions are no-nos). It would be helpful to obtain information about their typical clientele. For example, do they serve people who only have six-figure incomes? Most important, you should know how often they will contact you to review your financial progress.

There are a plethora of books and reading materials about investing that you can read on your own. Many people, especially those who are afraid to invest, may find these types of books boring. In the area of finances, there is nothing wrong with seeking professional help and advice. My goal is to get you immediately started by showing you what I did and giving you a basic explanation of the various investment categories.

Types of Investments

The general classes of investments are as follows:

Cash investments. These investments are short-term in nature—usually they mature in less than 120 days and are typically comprised of commercial paper, certificate of deposits, etc. U.S. treasury securities, which are short-term debt issued by governmental agencies, are in this category. These types of investments are considered safe because they are not sensitive to changes in interest rates, so they do not fluctuate in value. When you invest your money in these types of assets, the amount you invest, known as the principal, does not change in value. However, the interest on these investments is usually higher than what you would receive if you were to invest that money in a regular bank or credit union savings account.

Bonds. These are loan or debt instruments. When you buy a bond, you are lending the bond issuer your money. Bonds pay you, the lender, a certain amount of interest at specific times. They typically pay more interest than cash investments because you are taking on more risk. For example, if you purchase a ten-year bond from Ford Motor Company at an interest rate of 8 percent, what you are doing is lending them your money for ten years at an 8 percent interest rate. If the Ford Motor Company goes out of business, then you will not get your money back.

Usually, people who invest in bonds have a low to moderate risk tolerance level. Bond prices are determined by the risk level of the entity issuing the bond. So the more unstable the company, the lower the bond price will be to take into account the possibility that the company may not be able to repay your investment. However, the interest rate is typically higher to entice you, the investor, to buy the bond.

Conversely, the more solid a company, the lower the interest rate. The reason is you are basically assured that you will receive your principal investment along with the stated interest promised by the lender. There are many types of bonds: corporate bonds, which are bonds issued by corporations; municipal bonds, which are bonds funded by local governments; and U.S. savings bonds, which are bonds issued by the federal government.

Bonds also have different maturity levels. Short-term bonds mature in less than seven years. Bonds that generally mature within seven to fifteen years are considered intermediate-term bonds. Finally, long-term bonds are bonds that will come due in fifteen years or more. The longer the maturity of the bond, the more risky it is because the bond price is affected by the market interest rate.

Stocks. Stocks are shares of ownership in a company. One way a company can raise money is to sell stocks to the public and allow investors to own an interest in the company. This is how most investors build wealth. The goal is to buy shares in good companies whose stock value will increase over time.

Stocks can sell for pennies per share to more than one hundred dollars per share. A stock price is measured by the financial health of the company. The value of stocks change daily, which makes them, in general, riskier than bonds and cash investments.

As a shareholder, you are affected by the success or failure of the company that you invest in. So the more riskier the company, the more volatile the stock price. However, there is a possibility of receiving a huge rate of return on your investment in the company by taking on significant risk.

There are many types of stocks. Blue-chip stocks are stocks from high-quality, established companies. Examples of blue-chip companies include General Electric, IBM, and Coca-Cola. The prices for these stocks can be expensive because many investors want to own them due to a high confidence that the companies will not go out of business and will be profitable. There are also growth stocks where the companies who issue them invest their profits back into the company with the goal of increasing the company's performance and viability. High-tech companies, drug companies, and biotech companies are usually considered growth businesses. Growth stocks fluctuate significantly, which makes them risky, but they typically offer a higher rate of return than blue-chip stocks. You can also invest in stocks issued by non-U.S. companies, which are called international stocks. These can be very high-risk depending on the company and the market of the country where the company is based.

If your portfolio consists mostly of stocks, you would be considered an aggressive investor who is willing to take on a lot of risk. When you take substantial risks, you have a greater chance of a bigger return if the stock market goes up; but on the flip side, if the stock market goes down, your portfolio can suffer a huge hit. This is why investing in stocks is supposed to be for the long-term so that you can ride out any market downturns.

While you can invest in individual stocks, bonds, and cash investments, you may not want to spend your time deciding what to invest in. There are thousands upon thousands of different companies and businesses in which you can invest; but it would require an extensive amount of research that you probably do not have the time nor the inclination to do (I know I have better things to do with my time). There is another way to invest without having to select individual stocks or bonds. An investor can purchase mutual funds.

Investing in Mutual Funds

A *mutual fund* is a large pool of money contributed by investors to purchase investment products. The money is handled by a portfolio manager who researches, analyzes, and selects specific stocks, bonds, and/or cash investments to achieve a particular financial objective. In the financial world, investors are encouraged to spread their money through various types of investments. This concept is known as *diversification*.

When investing your money, you do not want to have "all your eggs in one basket"—a common phrase touted by financial experts. When your money is well diversified, you can obtain the highest possible rate of return on your money with the lowest amount of risk because all investments are not affected the same way on a daily basis in the stock market. So for instance, if you have your money invested in various types of stocks, if the share price of stock A goes down, it can be countered by a gain in stock B's price. If you add bond funds or cash investments to the mix, you are inoculating your investment portfolio against significant changes in value.

Mutual funds commonly invest in many different types of stock, bonds, and cash investments. There are also mutual funds that mimic various financial indices like the Standard & Poor's 500 (S&P 500) or Dow Jones Industrial Average (DJIA); hence, these types of mutual funds are known as index funds. Therefore, by investing in mutual funds, you secure the protections associated with diversification.

If your employer offers a retirement plan, you are given a list of a vast array of mutual funds in which you can invest. The funds range from various types of investments comprising of cash investments, stocks, and bonds. Check with your human resources department if you don't know whether your company offers a retirement plan for its employees.

If your job does not offer one, you can still invest your money in a retirement account. You can purchase mutual funds for your retirement at a brokerage firm, such as Vanguard, Fidelity Investments, and T. Rowe Price, to name a few. Each mutual fund has an investment goal, and the fund manager invests in a manner to best achieve the fund's objectives.

The types of investments that comprise a mutual fund are stated in a document called a prospectus. When I began selecting the mutual funds for my retirement account, I skimmed the prospectus. Frankly, I must admit, I found reading it to be quite boring. When I saw all the companies that a particular fund invested in, I felt comfortable knowing that my investments would be well diversified and that all my eggs certainly would not be in one basket.

When purchasing mutual funds, make sure that you buy no-load mutual funds. No-load funds do not charge sales commissions. If you pay a commission in order to buy a mutual fund, it reduces the amount that you will ultimately make on your investment. If you want to research a mutual fund that you are considering buying, go to *www.morningstar.com* for a fund rating. I think it is important for me to reiterate this: if doing this on your own makes you queasy, seek the help of a professional. Most mutual fund companies, if not all, provide professional assistance in selecting funds. You should feel free to call the fund company's toll free number for help.

Leaving With Your Retirement Money

Do not worry about losing the money that you invested in a 401(k) or 403(b) plan if you change jobs. If you leave your job, you will be able to take that money with you, transfer it into an IRA rollover account, and place it in your subsequent employer's plan. An IRA rollover account is an account that holds your retirement proceeds when you change jobs. If your next employer does not offer a retirement plan, then you can place the money in a retirement account with a brokerage firm. You do not want to have your employer issue you a check for your retirement proceeds if you were to leave your job because if you do not place the money in another retirement account by a certain time, you will face severe tax consequences. It is better to have your company directly transfer the money into a rollover account. The brokerage firm where you will establish your IRA rollover can handle this for you.

Beginning My Retirement Savings

When I first started my retirement investing, the question I had to ponder was how much money I was going to contribute. At the time, I was still an entry-level employee, had daily living expenses and a massive debt that I had needed to pay. So I decided to start small by having 5 percent of my gross pay taken from each paycheck and placed in a 401(k) account. If I determined that I could not handle that amount, I would reduce the amount of my contribution by 1 percent until I felt comfortable.

I will admit, I was a bit nervous when I received my first paycheck after joining the 401(k) plan. However, when I saw that my net paycheck did not change all that much, I realized that it was not a financial hardship to contribute to a retirement plan. What I discovered is that when you contribute to a 401(k) or any other employer-sponsored retirement plan, you are not taxed on the amount you contribute.

When I first started contributing to my 401(k), approximately $66 per paycheck was being deducted from my gross income. Had I not participated, it would not have meant that my paycheck would have been $66 higher. The $66 would have been taxed by the federal and state governments, so I probably would not have seen $20 of that money.

An additional bonus of contributing 5 percent of my gross income was that my taxable income was reduced by the amount of my contribution to my 401(k). As a result, my tax liability was lower due to my participating in my employer-sponsored retirement plan. So if your salary is $40,000 and you contribute 5 percent of your gross income ($2,000), your taxable income is $38,000.

As time went on, my salary increased modestly. As a result, the amount of my retirement contributions would automatically increase because I was contributing a percentage of my gross income. When I became comfortable with the amount I was contributing, I increased the amount of my contribution to 8 percent of my gross pay. A few years later, I increased my contribution to 10 percent. Currently, I contribute 15 percent of my gross salary to my 401(k).

I typically increase my contributions whenever I receive a raise. Since I was already living within my means, I figured that instead of having additional money from an increased paycheck blindly absorbed into my monthly expenses, I would use the pay raise to my advantage by directing it toward my long-term retirement savings. By doing this, I was benefiting by increasing the amount of my savings while remaining in a lower tax bracket. I am proud to say that this has been one of my best financial moves because years later, with the magic of compound interest, I have built quite a substantial nest egg for my retirement and have another thirty years to benefit from compounding until I reach retirement age. Compounding is basically interest building on the interest and contributions that you make to your retirement.

Having started investing in my retirement fund was a boost to my ego, especially when I began house hunting. I recommend that you begin contributing to a retirement plan before you purchase a home—if you are not already a homeowner. The reason is that you get a better picture on how much you really can afford for a house when you are actively funding a retirement account. With all the money that I had to pay for closing costs, it was nice knowing that I had money set aside and accruing for my retirement. (I will discuss home buying in the next chapter.)

Don't Fear the Stock Market

Some people find the whole stock market and concept of investing quite intimidating. All the numbers and symbols streaming on the bottom of a television screen can make you dizzy. I will be frank; I do not really pay attention to the stock market that much because I have a nicely diversified portfolio, and I currently invest 15 percent of my gross monthly pay consistently. Since I know that the stock market historically provides a rate of return of about 10 percent, I am confident that my money is working for me.

If the price of any stock drops, I will have, in my investment portfolio, an arsenal of stocks whose prices have increased. Additionally, I don't sweat it when the stock market falls because I benefit from a concept known as dollar cost averaging. *Dollar cost averaging* means that when stock prices are low, the amount of money I contribute to my retirement account allows me to buy more shares of stock. Conversely, when prices are high, I'm buying fewer stocks. Therefore, I am not faced with having to time the market by guessing when stock prices will rise and fall.

The Smart Investor

The key to a successful retirement savings is to start saving early and as aggressively as your stomach can handle. Make sure the money you invest is diversified among various types of stocks, bonds, and cash investments. You may want to select a couple of mutual funds offered by your employer-sponsored retirement plan and invest an equal amount in each just to get started. As you become accustomed to investing, you will probably feel more comfortable in reallocating your contributions to each mutual fund in a manner that reflects your risk tolerance level.

Many investment companies offer target maturity or life cycle mutual funds. These types of funds comprise of a different mix of stocks, bonds, and cash investments that are automatically changed or rebalanced over time to provide you with the best possible return with a low amount of risk based upon when you plan to retire. Remember, retirement savings are for the long haul. Know that as you save each month, the amount saved is being compounded with the previous amounts saved.

When determining how much you should invest and have deducted from each paycheck toward a retirement plan, I recommend you start small so that you get comfortable with the process of putting money aside. Various financial books suggest contributing the maximum amount of your salary that you are permitted by law. While that is certainly a lofty goal, it may not be practical, initially, for someone who has a low salary and high living expenses. That is not to say that you shouldn't strive for that goal—just don't do that to the detriment of any other financial goals that you may have.

If you want to learn more about investing, try *www.investorguide.com*. Also, for a great Web site to help you to start your retirement planning, go to *www.usatoday.com/money*. If you feel that you do not have any money to invest, try reducing your monthly expenses by 5 percent and invest that amount into a retirement plan. Another thing you can do, which is a practice that I have maintained, is when you get your next raise, funnel some, if not all, of the raise into a retirement account. The key is to get started because once you build momentum, there will be no stopping you.

Something else you can do to generate money to invest in your retirement is to increase the number of withholdings that you claim on your federal Form W-4. This will increase the amount of your paycheck. Take the increase and direct it into a retirement plan. Remember, you do not want to set yourself up for failure. Again, start small, invest methodically, and you are certain to succeed.

Unless you are approaching retirement age, I do not think it is necessary to determine how much you will actually need in retirement. The fact that you have begun to save puts you way ahead of the game. If you are approaching retirement age or are curious to know what you'll need when you retire, you can go on the Internet for help in planning your retirement. A good Web site that I recommend is operated by the American Savings Education Council at *www.asec.org*. On their Web site, you will find a link to their Ballpark E$timate worksheet that can help you determine how much you will need to save in order to retire comfortably. Another Web site that may be helpful in your retirement planning is *www.money.cnn.com*.

Individual Retirement Accounts

If your employer does not offer a retirement plan, you are not out of luck. As a wage earner, you have the option to invest in an Individual Retirement Account (IRA). The two most popular IRAs for you to consider are a traditional IRA and Roth IRA.

With both the traditional IRA and Roth IRA, the money is not taxed by the Internal Revenue Service (IRS) while it remains in the account. The difference between the Roth IRA and a traditional IRA is that with a traditional IRA, the money is taxed when it is withdrawn but not with a Roth IRA. In a Roth, all withdrawals made are tax free. Contributions to a traditional IRA can be deducted, up to certain limits, each year on your tax return. However, that is not the case with contributions made to a Roth IRA.

There are limits to the amount you can contribute to an IRA, which usually change each year. Those age fifty and over can contribute more than their younger counterparts, subject to certain limits as well. So if you are entering or desire to enter public interest legal work and are at least fifty years of age, you can catch up. If you contributed $6,000 a year at age fifty and if you retire at age sixty-five, you could accumulate over $150,000, assuming your retirement account averaged an interest rate of 9 percent—which is nothing to sneeze at especially if you have not started saving for retirement. Money that you place in an IRA grows tax free, allowing you to benefit from the compounding effect of the money that has accrued. If the money was taxed, it would not grow as much, which makes this a good investment vehicle.

I do not have an IRA, but I intend to open a Roth IRA when I turn forty. I like the fact that all monies contributed to a Roth IRA can be withdrawn even before I reach retirement age without any penalties. Also, I believe that I could likely be in a higher tax bracket when I reach retirement, so I like the fact that any money withdrawn from a Roth IRA is not taxed. What I also learned is that, with traditional IRA contributions, you must begin withdrawing your money at age 70 ½; and you can no longer contribute to a traditional IRA. But this rule does not apply to a Roth IRA. Therefore, in my opinion, I believe that you get a better deal if you invest in a Roth IRA as opposed to a traditional IRA. If you are not sure which way to go, I suggest you consult a financial planner who can assess your personal situation and provide you with the proper advice.

Don't Touch It!

Retirement savings is just for that—retirement. If you withdraw money prior to reaching retirement age, you are subject to a 10 percent early withdrawal penalty, and the amount withdrawn is subject to federal and state taxes. There are several exceptions for early withdrawals, within certain limits, from a retirement plan. You can withdraw money for the purchase of a home, to handle emergency medical expenses, or to pay for higher education costs. As I just mentioned, there are no early withdrawal penalties for contributions made to a Roth IRA.

If you need to withdraw your retirement money early, see an accountant to assess how that will impact your tax liability. But I advise you not to touch your retirement money for any reason (unless you decide to retire). The way to increase your wealth is by having the money in your retirement account compound for as long as possible. The longer the compounding, the better. Every year, I have seen how my retirement money has grown. Touching that money, for me, is out of the question.

I encourage you to be patient with the growth of your retirement money. It's not wise to withdraw money or close your retirement account because the stock market is declining. The history of the stock market has shown that it will rebound. Keep in mind, you are investing for the long-term in a retirement plan. Therefore, you have time to weather any storms. I rarely look at my retirement account balance when the stock market goes down. I really do not need the stress. However, if you feel you must look, look at your retirement account only when the stock market is doing well. Usually when the stock market hits a record high, I sneak a peek at my retirement account for a confidence boost. I always like what I see, which gives me the encouragement I need to continue investing for the long haul.

Hopefully, I have convinced you to start investing in your retirement. You will be so glad that you did. Starting your retirement investing now will give you so many options on how you can spend your retirement years.

Action Plan

1. Determine how much you will contribute to your retirement plan.

2. Contact your human resources department and complete a retirement account application.

    a. If your employer does not offer a retirement plan, contact a discount brokerage firm and open an Individual Retirement Account.

3. Select the funds offered by the retirement plan that you want your money invested in.

4. Review your investment allocation every six months.

5. Increase your contributions until you are investing at least 10 percent of your gross income.

6. Do not withdraw your money until you reach retirement age.

CHAPTER 5
$ $ $ $

Buying And Owning A Home
Attain the American Dream

Oh, the joy of homeownership! This is what many consider the ultimate American Dream. If you want to purchase a home and believe that your public interest salary makes it unattainable, then read on. Despite what you may think, you can work at a legal services organization and own a lovely home.

I will be the first to admit that I did not think it was possible to be a homeowner on the salary of a public interest attorney unless you had a spouse who was gainfully employed or were able to find a roommate to help pay the mortgage. The down payment alone on a modest home scared the living daylights out of me. Although I prided myself on saving money from each paycheck, I thought that I would be ninety years old before I came close to saving enough money for a down payment. But I can remember when, at the age of thirty-two, on a snowy and ice-filled day in February of 2003, I received the keys to my first new home; and I have been a homeowner ever since—without a roommate!

To Buy or Not to Buy

I want to state that buying a home is not necessarily for everyone. There are solid reasons why one should rent as opposed to own. For one thing, when you own a home, you are responsible for all the repairs, maintenance, and upkeep—which does not come cheap. But when you rent, the landlord must make the repairs. Also, renting allows you more flexibility in your ability to move as opposed to owning a home. If you decide that you want to move, as a renter, you can let the landlord know that you will not renew the lease and simply move out. However, it is not that easy when you want to move from a home that you own—especially if you are trying to sell it in what is deemed to be a slow market. The cost, time, and energy in selling a home can keep you tied down to a particular location longer than you may like. But if you really want to own a home on a public interest attorney's salary, it is possible.

After a few years of renting an apartment in suburban Baltimore, I knew it was time for me to buy a house because I decided to make Maryland my home. Whether you rent or own, you can still have a beautiful place to lay your head, all on a public interest attorney's salary; and I will tell you how I did it. The principles and steps that I utilized, which propelled me from renter to homeowner, can be applied even with a modest income. If you believe renting is best for you, you can lease a nice place on a legal aid salary. It all boils down to doing your homework so that you can get the best possible place that you can afford.

The Road to Homeownership

My first job out of law school was working as a law clerk for a Baltimore City Circuit Court judge. At that time, the pay was less than the starting salary of most public interest attorney positions—so I really had to work hard to find a nice yet affordable apartment. Even in law school, I was accustomed to living in a nice space. I grew up in a nice home with a room of my own. So there was no way I was going to settle for less. Since my income was really limited, I had to scrutinize how I was going to spend my money. I had to assess my Spending Plan and determine where I could make some changes.

When I began house hunting, I made the amount of my monthly rent my initial target goal for my home mortgage payment primarily because I thought it would be manageable. I did a lot of research and reading before I purchased my first home. A must read, in my opinion, for anyone seeking to purchase a home is *Home Buying for Dummies*. I learned that a mortgage payment generally comprises of not only the principal and interest but also includes property taxes and homeowner's insurance. Therefore, there was no guarantee that even if you had a fixed-rate mortgage, your mortgage payments would always be the same during the life of the mortgage loan.

People in the real estate business, in touting the benefits of homeownership to renters, often state that if you buy a home, you don't have to worry about your mortgage increasing—unlike when you rent. But that is a bit misleading because if your property taxes and homeowner's insurance increases, then your housing payment goes up. So whether you rent or decide to own, you can surely count on your housing payments to change. However, I will say that since I purchased my home, my mortgage payment has not risen to the extent that my rent used to increase each year. I am convinced that, if I still rented the same one-bedroom apartment I had before owning a home, I would be paying more in rent than what I am currently paying on my home mortgage.

After determining my initial target mortgage goal, I then looked at all of my monthly expenses and realistically scrutinized whether I could adjust my expenses so that I could accommodate a higher mortgage payment. This is where I really had to get real. I had no intention of living on a diet of bread and water in order to pay a mortgage. Also, I was not willing to forgo luxury vacations in order to make a huge monthly mortgage payment. Essentially, I was not willing to sacrifice my personal value of having a quality life in order to buy a home.

Keeping in step with my values, I determined that my maximum monthly mortgage payment could be no higher than $850. This amount included property taxes and homeowner's insurance. I held firm to that number and was willing to continue renting if I could not find a nice house with a mortgage payment of $850 or less. I then used a mortgage calculator to determine the purchase price of homes where the mortgage payment would not be above $850 per month. I recommend that you use any of the available free online mortgage calculators by googling *mortgage calculators* to help determine the highest purchase price that you can spend on a home by combining your desired mortgage payment and the most favorable interest rate you can obtain. Once you have done this, you can start looking for a realtor.

Finding a Realtor

I began interviewing prospective realtors, who were referred by friends and colleagues, and told them what I was looking for—a completely finished three-level townhouse with at least two bedrooms and two bathrooms with a mortgage payment no higher than $850 per month. Of the realtors I interviewed, only one believed that I could find a house with the monthly mortgage payment that I was seeking. I selected that individual to be my realtor. What I learned, through my realtor, was that the most important thing was to get a really low-interest rate mortgage. It is amazing how a one-tenth difference in an interest rate can significantly affect a mortgage payment amount. So I was scouring the Internet and newspapers to see which mortgage companies and banks were offering very low interest rates.

Searching for a Mortgage

While seeking a competitive mortgage, an obstacle that I had to overcome was obtaining money for a down payment. At the time I was house hunting, I really did not have money for a down payment. I had emergency savings of $3,000, but it was for just that—emergencies. I really did not want to touch that money because I wanted to have it available for any unexpected repairs that I would have to make to my house once I bought it.

Fortunately, there are many mortgages out there that do not require a down payment. However, many prospective home buyers will have to pay something called private mortgage insurance (PMI) if they pay less than a 20 percent down payment for a home. The PMI will be included into the mortgage payment, which can impact how much house you can ultimately afford.

I continued to search for a good mortgage rate. Not only did I find a mortgage directed to first-time home buyers where I was not required to make a down payment, but I also did not have to pay PMI. The mortgage interest rate that I found was very competitive at 6.75 percent. As a result, I was able to look at higher-priced homes because I no longer had to factor PMI into my monthly mortgage payment, and the interest rate I secured was low.

Even though realtors will help you find a mortgage, they really do not work for you or look after your best interests as the home buyer. The reason is that real estate agents get paid when the house is sold. The higher the sales price, the higher the realtor's commission. As a result, they really work for the seller.

Similarly, for securing a competitive mortgage, mortgage brokers really do not care if you can or cannot afford a home loan because they get paid when you obtain a loan from them. It also is common for mortgage lenders to sell your mortgage to another lender. Many realtors have business relationships with mortgage brokers with the main goal of earning their commissions at your expense. So it pays to do your own homework when searching and making an offer on a home, along with securing a competitive mortgage loan.

My primary search method for finding a mortgage loan was the Internet, which has a wealth of information about lenders and special offers for new home buyers. The primary Web site that I used to get information on mortgages was *www.bankrate.com* and *www.lendingtree.com*. I also googled *Baltimore mortgages* to see what popped up. You can do the same for the city in which you live. I called all the companies that I was interested in to get information about the mortgage offers to see if what they were advertising was legitimate. I made sure everything was in writing to prevent any miscommunication and to know exactly what I was getting into.

After careful and thorough research, I selected and was preapproved for a home loan through Baltimore American Mortgage Company. I obtained a home mortgage loan where I locked into a thirty-year fixed-rate loan at an interest rate of 6.75 percent. I did not have to come up with a down payment, and I did not have to pay PMI. I did have to contribute approximately $3,500 toward my closing costs, but I got $600 back at closing from my lender.

When I signed all the papers and received the keys to my new home, my mortgage payment was $877 per month. Now you may be saying that is $27 more than the maximum monthly mortgage payment of $850 that I said I was willing to pay. While that is true, you should know that during the house-hunting process, I received a pay raise at work and, as a result, was willing to go slightly over my targeted maximum monthly mortgage payment.

Types of Mortgages

One thing about mortgages is that there are so many different types. You can get a fixed-rate loan where the interest rate remains the same during the life of the loan. There are adjustable rate mortgages (also known as ARMs) where the interest rate changes. You can also get a mortgage that has an interest rate that is both fixed and adjustable, commonly known as a hybrid loan. A prospective home buyer can obtain an interest-only mortgage loan and only be required to pay the interest on the principal balance for a specified period of time. Another mortgage is a balloon mortgage where you pay a monthly mortgage payment for a certain time, and then the full balance of the mortgage loan all comes due on a particular date. Balloon mortgages are very dangerous, and I do not recommend them.

Regardless of your salary, I suggest that you stick with a fixed-rate loan. The reason why I am in favor of fixed-rate mortgages is that you know what your payments are going to be. If you get an adjustable rate mortgage, when interest rates rise, so does your mortgage payment. Conversely, if interest rates are lowered, then your mortgage payments will be lowered. But why go through the roller coaster of emotions regarding your mortgage payments if you don't have to?

The homes of many holders of adjustable rate mortgages went into foreclosure because they could not make their payments when the interest rates began to rise. Interest only loans are a big rip-off because you continually make mortgage payments, but your principal loan balance never goes down. In my humble opinion and experience, it is important to keep things simple with your finances. I cannot think of any better situation to keep things uncomplicated with your money when buying a house than by going with a fixed-rate loan.

Have only one mortgage on your home. Do not take out a second mortgage. I get all these offers to open a second mortgage, home equity loan, or home equity line of credit. All that these loans do is get you into additional debt by using the equity in your home. Equity is the difference between a home's fair market value and the mortgage balance. The loans are secured through a lien on your house. If you fail to pay any of these additional mortgage loans, the lender will be able to foreclose on your house. It's really not worth it.

Home Buying Programs

Also, note that there are special loans for home buyers who have modest salaries and work in certain types of fields. These loans can pay part, if not all, of your down payment and closing costs. Closing costs are those fees independent of your down payment and are associated with buying a home. Closing costs average 3.5 percent of the purchase price of a home and include administrative costs, appraisal fees, credit report fees, prorated property taxes, home insurance premiums, recording and title fees, to name a few.

Many of these special home buyer loans offer interest rates that are below market value. For some, these loans are beneficial. But you have to be very careful when taking on these types of loans because they contain many restrictions, such as how long you must reside in the home or whether you can rent your home to another person. Also, some of the loans restrict the kind of neighborhoods you can choose to live in order to obtain the loan. I considered getting one but ultimately decided that it did not suit me, and I still fared well with a conventional mortgage.

Obtaining the American Dream

I realize housing prices can vary throughout the country. There are states that have exorbitant home prices. However, there are public interest attorneys in all areas of the United States who own homes and are able to take advantage of various home-buying programs targeted for lower-income earners. Therefore, there is really no reason why you can't be a homeowner if that is what you really want.

I suggest you consider doing what I did and look at what you currently pay in rent as a starting point (provided that your rent payments are manageable). If you still live at home with your parents, relatives, or benevolent friends who do not charge you rent (lucky you), use your money to save for a really hefty down payment. Establish a Spending Plan based on your values to come up with a mortgage payment that you would feel comfortable paying.

If you get paid biweekly or bimonthly, your first paycheck of the month, after you pay yourself first, should be able to cover your mortgage and utilities (gas, electric, and phone). You definitely do not want your mortgage payment to consume your entire first paycheck and a portion of your second paycheck of the month. If it does, you are setting yourself up for trouble, and your quality of life will definitely suffer.

I am really glad that I stuck to my guns and did not compromise on what I was willing to pay for my home. I did not want to be "house poor." In the past few years after purchasing my house, I have received several modest raises and a promotion at my job. This has enabled me to pay extra toward my mortgage principal every year.

Also, I have been able to decorate my home because I have discretionary money available. Shortly after buying my home, I personally designed and had custom-built a home office and entertainment center in the lower level of my home. (I felt like a celebrity!) Additionally, by being honest about what I could afford, I have been able to hire a landscaper to cut and edge my lawn on a weekly basis. I have purchased stainless steel appliances in my kitchen and undergone additional home improvement projects.

After a long hard day at work, I come home to a beautiful and tastefully decorated house. When people compliment me on my home, it feels really good to show them how a single person can be a homeowner on the salary of a public interest attorney. I am proof that if you want to be a homeowner, you certainly can!

Action Plan

1. Open a credit union, money market, or online bank account and start saving monthly for a home.

2. Determine the maximum mortgage payment that you can afford.

3. Locate a low fixed-rate mortgage loan, which requires the lowest possible down payment.

4. Find a realtor to help you find a home that is within your price range based upon your desired mortgage payment and the lowest interest rate that you qualify for.

5. Look only at those homes within your desired price range.

6. Once you find the home that is right for you, make an offer and buy it!

7. Make an extra payment toward your mortgage principal each year.

CHAPTER 6
$ $ $ $
Eliminating Credit Card Debt
Get Out of the Debt Trap

I remember it clearly; it was about ten thirty in the evening on December 31, 2005. While people were getting dressed up to go out and ring in the New Year, I put on some jeans and sweats and drove to my local post office. I entered into the parking lot and proceeded to the mailbox. I reached into my purse and grabbed my last credit card bill payment. I rolled down the window and dropped the payment in the mailbox. I then got out of my car and started dancing. I was so elated because I finally had no more credit card debt. For the first time in over a decade, I would be bringing in the New Year without any credit card debt. My hard work paid off, and I felt so light and free. I danced so much that I did not realize that I was blocking a man in a minivan who pulled up behind me in order to drop his mail. He must have thought that I was crazy. But I did not care. All I knew was that my credit card debt was gone, and I was overjoyed.

Are you carrying boatloads of credit card debt? Do you feel that your public interest salary is preventing you from getting free from debt? Is your debt making you feel that you can't achieve your financial goals? Well, I am here to tell you how to knock out those credit card debts once and for all.

How the Credit Card Debt Began

For so many years, I was very ignorant about my dependence on credit cards. I had so many cards. Not only did I have the major credit cards such as MasterCard, Visa, and Discover, I had an American Express Card and credit cards from all the major department stores like Lord & Taylor, Bloomingdale's, and Macy's. I was even a credit card carrier of small mall stores like Bath & Body Works and the Limited Express.

Despite having all these credit cards, I was constantly receiving offers in the mail to open up new credit accounts. As a result, I had multiple Visa cards and MasterCards, and I used them all. Even still, I did not believe that I abused credit cards. I rarely purchased big-ticket items on my credit card. I'm not into electronic gadgets, so I was not buying big-screen televisions.

But my credit card debt would creep up when I charged dinners out with friends. I love clothes and felt that I needed to look like a professional. As a result, I would charge a substantial amount of work clothes and justified the purchases because I bought them on "sale." Whenever my car needed repair, I would just whip out the credit card. It was not unusual for me to charge my groceries. My logic was since I was buying things that I "needed," I was being responsible with my credit. However, that was not true.

Regardless of the purchase, I was spending more than I was earning and was always in the red. This prevented me from being able to save my money because any discretionary money I had was going to pay my credit card debt. When the bills came, I would gasp. I had estimated in my mind how much I charged on each card during any thirty-day period, but the numbers on the credit card statements did not match the numbers in my head. I would think, *There must be some mistake*, and I would review each and every line item of my credit card statements to make sure the amounts were correct. I would add it all up, and without fail, the credit card statements were accurate.

I would then tell myself that I will never again charge so much and would write a "large" check in order to reduce the credit card bill. Then it would not even be halfway through the month when I would run out of cash and have to resort to using my credit cards again. I would rationalize and say, "Well, I paid a big chunk of money down, so a little purchase here and there will not hurt. After all, life is short." But when I received the next credit card statement, it would be higher than the previous month.

Since I had so many different credit cards with varying balances, I never knew what my total credit card debt was. I must admit, I really did not want to know. However, when I decided to get control over my money, I took a calculator and a deep breath and added up my total credit card debt. It was over $10,000! I couldn't believe it. When I saw that number, it was my rock bottom, and that's when I decided that something really had to change.

Conquering the Credit Monster

I decided that I was going to pay off my credit card debt and save money at the same time. Since I got into credit card debt through a series of small purchases over time, I decided to employ that same strategy to get out of debt and build my savings. I realized that I did not accumulate the debt overnight, so I was not going to eliminate it overnight. I was going to have to take it slow and easy. As I paid my debt, my discretionary income began to increase. As a result, I was able to save more.

The way I began tackling my credit card debt was by gradually decreasing my dependence on them. I used my credit cards on practically everything imaginable. Credit cards were used even if I had the cash to pay for it. So I had to wean myself off of them.

Many financial experts advise people in credit card debt to go cold turkey and stop using their credit cards altogether. While logically, that is an excellent idea, most people are unable to do it. It is like people who want to lose weight and are told to go on an extreme diet by eating nothing but water and crackers. If you do that, you will likely lose a lot of weight, but within days, you will feel so deprived that you go crazy and eat everything in sight, sabotaging your weight-loss efforts. Instead of losing weight, more pounds are packed back on. What I find the financial experts forget is that things happen, and it's called life: the car breaks down, and you need to pay for a major repair; a loved one becomes seriously ill, and you have to catch a plane to be with family; your washing machine no longer works, and you have to replace it. I can go on and on, but I think you get the point.

When I decided that I wanted to be free from credit card debt, I wanted it to be for good. So like my savings plan, I started small. Instead of saying that I was not going to use my credit cards anymore, I reviewed my spending and decided that I would not use credit cards to pay for gas for my car. I thought that was a reasonable expense that I could handle. I did that for a few months and then took another expense, such as movies and eating out, and started paying cash or using my debit card for those purchases in addition to paying cash for gas.

The more I did this, the less I became dependent on credit cards. As a result, I saw my confidence rising on my ability to manage my money. My overall debt started to gradually decrease, along with the minimum required credit payments. As a result, I started having more cash at my disposal, which I used to further my financial goals.

Taking My Head Out of the Sand

My road to financial prosperity began with being honest and facing the music about my debt. The only way I could do this was to know how much I owed on all of my credit cards. It was not easy, but it also was not as hard to do because I had already addressed my student loan debt.

For most law students, student loan debt is their largest liability, which is why I urge you to address that debt immediately. As I mentioned, the decision to remain ignorant about my credit card debt was tempting as I had credit balances spread amongst different credit cards. The thought of knowing the total amount was quite frightening. What got me through this was putting this whole debt thing into perspective. I could not give it more power than it truly deserved. It was just that—debt. Yes, I owed money. However, it was just one aspect of my multifaceted life. I've heard countless stories of people getting out of massive debt without having to file for bankruptcy, and there was not anything remarkably special about them. So I vowed that if they could do it, I could as well.

Regardless of how long it took to pay off my credit card debt, I made sure not to deprive myself of life's pleasures in the process. My plan was to start small and be consistent in paying down my debt while saving money to have fun and enjoy my life. I knew I could only do this if I calculated all of my debt to know where I stood. So I did just that; I added it up, took a break, and went out to catch a movie and enjoy a dessert. I wanted to celebrate the courageous act of tabulating my credit card debt.

This is what I want you to do right now: put down this book and write down all of your debt (don't include student loan debt or your mortgage balance, if you have one). Be sure to include any debt owed to family and friends. Take a deep breath and add up your total. Exhale. Put your pen or pencil down and go out and treat yourself to something nice in celebration of this major step you just took to get out of debt. . . .

. . . Now I hope you just did something nice for yourself and that you have resumed reading this book because you are now ready to take action to pay off your credit card debt. The first thing you need to do is list each of your debts in order, from the smallest to largest balance. You might have heard financial gurus talk about listing your debts in order by interest rate—largest to smallest—and tackle the highest interest rate credit card debt first. I'll admit you will save more money in interest payments if you do it that way. However, if the debt that has the highest interest rate has a balance of $58,000, it could take you several years before you pay that off. But if you saw yourself eliminating the smaller debts in a few months, you are more likely to stick to methodically paying down your credit card debt. It's like being on a weight-loss plan and having to wait months to see one pound drop off. You are more apt to stick to a diet if you start to see results quickly in the beginning.

If you would rather conquer your debt by starting with the largest interest rate first as opposed to the smallest loan balance, be my guest. While I personally prefer eliminating credit card debt from the smallest to largest amount owed, do what works for you. The choice is yours so long as you are making monthly payments to reduce all of your debt.

Now, along with each debt listed, write the minimum amount you are required to pay on each and total that up. Say for instance, your debt is as follows:

Creditor	Balance	Minimum Payment
Sears	$ 500.00	$ 20.00
MasterCard	$1,125.00	$ 45.00
Discover Card	$2,375.00	$ 95.00
Visa	$3,250.00	$130.00
Total	**$7,250.00**	**$290.00**

Your total minimum monthly payment due in this example is $290. You will pay at least the minimum payments on each of the cards. When the $500 Sears balance is paid off, you will then apply the $20 minimum payment you had been paying on your Sears card to the MasterCard balance and make minimum monthly payments of $65 ($20 + $45) until that is paid off and then add the $65 monthly MasterCard payments to the $95 minimum payment to the Discover Card and so on. You will do this until all of your credit card debt is paid off. If you haven't included your credit card debt payments in your Spending Plan, now is definitely the time to do so. You may likely have to shave off expenses in other spending categories so that you can meet your minimum payments.

Ratcheting Up the Ante

If you find that you can pay more than the minimum payment, by all means do so. I certainly did. What I did was multiply my total minimum payment by 10 percent and pay that additional amount toward my lowest credit balance to accelerate the payoff. Applying this concept to the above example, 10 percent of $290 is $29. You would add $29 to the $20 minimum payment on the Sears card and pay $49 each month until the credit bill was paid off. Afterward, you would apply the $49 to the minimum payment on the MasterCard until that credit card is paid off. If something happened and you couldn't pay $49 toward the Sears card, you would just pay the $20 minimum required.

During those months when I received three paychecks, I would take a portion of the third check of the month and apply a chunk of money to my credit card debt. But remember, if you decide to pay more than the minimum, make sure your Spending Plan still includes putting money toward pleasurable purchases and activities so that you don't feel as if you are depriving yourself as you pay down your debt.

After each month of making your payments, you will find that your minimum payments will decrease, which will begin to increase your cash flow. This will come in handy when preparing your Spending Plan for the next month because you will now have more discretionary money as a result of lower minimum payments. You may find, in creating your next Spending Plan, that certain expenses will increase due to periodic expenses (i.e., car insurance) coming due, and you do not have any or enough reserve savings to handle this. If that is the case, you may want to just pay the minimum on all your credit cards so that you can pay any nonrecurring expenses and then resume paying additional money toward your lowest credit balance in the subsequent month.

Talking to Your Creditors

If your debt far exceeds your ability to make even the minimum payment, I would urge you contact your creditors to see if they are willing to accept less than the minimum payment. Be candid with your creditors and let them know your circumstances and what you are able to pay. You would be surprised how much they are willing to negotiate. The earlier you let them know that you are trying to make good on what you owe them, the better.

It takes a lot of strength and fortitude to deal with your creditors because some can be downright nasty. When that happens, ask to speak to a manager. While you are in the process of negotiating with your creditors, continue to pay them something. The longer they see that you are sincere in your efforts to repay them, the less likely they will take legal action against you because it is a major expense to them if they have to sue to collect their money. You can also contact Consumer Credit Counseling Services (CCCS) for help. CCCS is a nonprofit organization that will negotiate with your creditors to create a workable repayment arrangement.

It Pays to Shop Around

One thing that I did when I was paying off my credit cards was to get my interest rate lowered. You can shop around for low-interest rate credit cards by checking out *www.bankrate.com* or *www.cardweb.com*. The lower the interest rate, the more quickly I was able to pay off my debt. At one point, I was able to reduce my interest rate to 0 percent for a specific period of time. When the promotional or "teaser" rate expired, I applied for another 0 percent credit card and transferred my balances.

A word of caution, many of these cards have universal default provisions (which, personally, I find despicable). Universal default means that if you are late with any of your creditors, you lose whatever promotional rate another creditor has given you. Even if you do not have a promotional rate on your credit cards, your creditors could still increase your interest rates with universal default. Therefore, you must make sure that you are on time with your payments to all of your creditors.

A good way to pay on time and avoid late fees is by paying your credit bills at least five days before they are due. I normally pay my bills online and print out a confirmation. You should also be aware that opening and closing numerous credit cards can negatively impact your credit score—which is what creditors look at when they decide to loan you money, issue you credit, and determine your interest rate. On the other hand, you should be aware that reducing your overall debt, along with developing a history of on-time payments, will improve your score.

Credit Cards as ATM Cards

Cash advances from your credit cards are no-nos and should be avoided, if possible, at all costs. There are fees assessed for getting a cash advance. Also, the interest rates are ridiculously high for cash advances. There is no grace period on the money taken out. So once you receive cash against your credit limit, the interest charged starts immediately. If you are currently making payments on credit cards where you have taken a cash advance, either pay it off immediately if you have the money to do so or transfer the balance to a credit card with a low or 0 percent interest rate.

The Result of Credit Card Independence

Interestingly, as I slowly began to use cash for more and more purchases, I started to see how I began spending differently. There is something about using cold, hard cash to buy things as opposed to using a credit card. This is how I really began to recognize what is truly important to me. If for example, I only had $30 in my wallet, and I am five days away from payday, spending $22.95 for a vase at a home furnishings store no longer made sense to me. However, if the vase was something I really wanted, I would wait until I got my paycheck and buy it. More often than not, I no longer desired the item anymore.

I became even more discerning in my spending as I saw my credit card balances go down. My motivation to save money toward various financial goals significantly increased. An important goal for me was to have an emergency savings account to handle the unexpected without having to resort to using my credit cards. As a result of reducing credit card debt, I was able to regularly fund an emergency savings account.

Handling Credit Card Setbacks and Surprises

Don't throw in the towel if you suffer a financial setback, which requires you to incur additional credit card debt. Debt repayment is a journey that sometimes will be smooth and, at other times, be bumpy. I cannot count how many times I would be riding high in my debt elimination process and then all of a sudden, the unexpected would occur (usually involving my house or car), and I would have to use my credit cards. But I remained determined to get out of debt and would just modify my Spending Plan to get back on track.

I used my setbacks as an opportunity to create new financial goals and review my Spending Plan. For instance, for several years, I owned a car that had to undergo major repairs. It was wreaking havoc on my monthly Spending Plan, which ultimately forced me to use my credit cards whenever car problems surfaced. As a result, I opened a savings account at a credit union for car repairs. Each month, I would deposit some of my saved change in that account. Also, whenever I got paid, I would deposit some money—even as low as $5—into my car repair account. My goal was to have the account reach $1,000. I achieved that goal fairly easily, and now when my car needs to be repaired, I don't have to resort to credit cards.

How I Use Credit Cards Now

While I still use my credit cards, I am not dependent on them. They are now used for convenience because I really don't like carrying a lot of cash. Since I compare my daily spending list to my Spending Plan on a weekly basis, I know where I stand in any particular spending category and will not use credit cards to sabotage myself financially. The years it took to pay down and eliminate my credit card debt taught me a valuable lesson on the dangers of improper credit card use and living above my means. It is a lesson that I don't want to repeat.

You will see how easy it becomes to rapidly achieve your financial goals by not having credit card debt. For me, it has made paydays more enjoyable. Eliminating credit card debt contributes to peace of mind and an increased quality of life because you are able to focus on what is important to you without worrying about debt.

Action Plan

1. Add up all of your credit card debt (include money owed to family and friends).

2. List each of your debts from the smallest to the largest balance.

3. Pay the minimum on your credit card debt except for the card that has the lowest balance.

4. For the card with the lowest balance, pay a little extra in addition to the minimum payment.

5. When the lowest credit card balance is paid off, apply the amount you had been paying to the next smallest card's minimum payment.

6. Follow steps 3-5 until your credit card debt is paid off.

7. Do your best not to charge additional credit card debt.

CHAPTER 7
$ $ $ $

Handling Financial Setbacks
Don't Give Up

As you go through the process of taking control of the money you earn as a public interest attorney and using it to achieve what matters most to you, you will face obstacles. I want to urge you not to give up. Encountering roadblocks does not mean that you can't make it on a legal aid salary. There will be times when you are riding high and are getting close to your financial goals, and then you suffer a financial setback.

I'll share with you a great example. While writing this book, I was doing well and began recovering from having to spend several thousands of dollars to get new underground plumbing in my home. Shortly after, I took my car for a regular oil change and learned that my car needed almost $3,000 worth of repairs! At the time, I was driving a thirteen-year-old Honda Civic and planned on holding it for another seven years. (Don't laugh, I really planned to own that car for twenty years before buying another car.)

My plan was, beginning in 2008, to save approximately $300 per month for the next six years to buy a new car. Well, that plan went up in smoke when the mechanic told me all the problems with my car. There was no way that I was going to put $3,000 into a car that old that may last another year or two, if I was lucky. So guess what? I had to go car shopping.

Since I was not prepared to buy a new car outright, I had to review my Spending Plan to find a way to purchase a new car. I could have used my car problems as an excuse to throw in the towel. But I took a deep breath, assessed my money situation, revisited my financial values, and did some car-buying research. Eventually, I bought a new car that was both reliable and affordable.

Another setback that I suffered was when my basement flooded a few years ago. At that time, I was at the halfway mark toward my goal of having $10,000 in my emergency savings account. The cost of having to pay a home restoration company to remove the water and clean my basement, in addition to buying and installing new carpet, practically wiped out my emergency savings. I was fortunate to have money saved to handle the problem without going into credit card debt. However, I was upset that I now had to start from scratch and rebuild my emergency savings. Nevertheless, I persevered and modified my Spending Plan to allocate more money to my emergency savings account.

No One Is Immune from Problems

Maybe in the course of your financial journey, you will not have to buy another car or restore a flooded basement. However, there are so many other things that can happen to derail the best of plans. You or your loved one can be diagnosed with a serious medical illness, which can result in having to pay for expensive medicine that is not covered by your health insurance. An uninsured careless driver hits your car, and you have to pay a large expense so that your car can be fixed. Your home needs a new roof, and you do not have enough cash to cover the repair.

There are so many unforeseen events that can thwart your plans for your money. I have been there. Keep in mind, it is your financial goals and values that will ground you and be the springboard for all the decisions that you make when handling your money. It is my firm belief that these setbacks are going to make you stronger and build character in order to make your money work for you in the best possible way.

Handling Setbacks

It is important to have a plan of attack on how you are going to handle unexpected events and emergencies as you fund your various goal savings accounts, invest for retirement, and pay off credit card and student loan debt. You may find yourself having to resort to credit cards to help you get through a challenging setback. If that is the case, do not beat yourself up. Remember, life happens and you have to go with the flow.

Credit card use, while it can be a quick fix, should be the last resort. If you end up incurring additional debt, you will just need to modify your Spending Plan for a few months to repay what you had to charge on your credit card in order to get back on track. I have done it and survived.

Another way to deal with setbacks is to make friends and develop relationships with people who are trying to get out of their financial traps and improve their money situation. Having a support system does wonders when you feel weak and want to throw in the towel after suffering a financial setback. My cousin, Brigitt, is my biggest supporter. We often discuss our financial dreams and goals with one another. Without fail, we are always there for one another to brainstorm solutions and to provide words of encouragement to get us through difficult times and to stay on course with our individual financial goals. I have met other attorneys at my office who share my same passion of achieving financial freedom and are doing their best to make their money stretch while having fun at the same time. Trust me, if you look around, you will find people who share similar financial goals and can provide money saving tips, especially when you face a financial obstacle.

On the flip side, you may want to steer clear of folks who can sabotage your financial goals. It may be intentional or unintentional on their part, based upon what is going on in their own financial lives. Friends and family, while meaning well, can sometimes provide the worst money advice—especially if they are struggling to stay afloat with their own finances. In my opinion, this is when you really have to demonstrate courage and hold firm to your values and keep your eyes on the prize. You will find that there are certain people with whom you cannot go to the mall with because they will encourage you to buy things that you really do not need or want. The motives can vary, but the bottom line is you do not want to be influenced to do things that will hurt you financially. In all things, including your finances, the choice is yours on how you either spend or invest your money.

Rising Above Setbacks

As you continue to follow your financial plan, you will find that it will begin to get easier. When I review all of my financial accounts and see how my investment and savings have grown over the years, I have to blink to make sure I am not seeing things. I can't believe how much I have accomplished financially despite the setbacks that I have experienced. The key is to stay the course and not give up.

Sometimes setbacks also can get you to reassess your Spending Plan to determine whether it is realistic. If you find yourself repeatedly overspending in a particular budget category, it can give you valuable insight to decide whether your goals and values have shifted. There is nothing wrong if your values and goals change because that means that you are growing as an individual. The whole idea is to engage in the work you love as a public interest attorney while thriving on your modest salary.

Any financial obstacle can be overcome. You are bound to make mistakes (I've made my fair share). Being clear on where you financially stand at the present moment and where you are heading will give you the power to go the distance. All I ask is that you don't give up!

Action Plan

1. Identify at least one person to be your financial "buddy".

2. When faced with a financial obstacle or setback, brainstorm ideas to solve the problem and enlist the help of your financial buddy if necessary.

3. Review your Spending Plan to pay for any out-of-pocket costs incurred to attack the problem.

4. Don't give up!

CONCLUSION
Cultivating an Attitude of Gratitude

I hope you have begun implementing the Action Plan strategies at the end of each chapter for managing your public interest salary. If you haven't, please get started! It is never too late to start using your salary as a public interest attorney to propel you toward financial freedom and achieving your money goals. There is no question that your life will begin to change.

I would be remiss if I did not mention that while you go through the process of managing your money, it is important to have an attitude of gratitude. While I certainly would not mind earning more money, I am thankful for what I do make as it has allowed me to accomplish numerous goals and increase my overall quality of life. When I see how the clients we assist at the Legal Aid Bureau, as well as the clients served by other legal services organizations, continually struggle for the basic necessities of life—such as food, clothing, decent housing, and affordable healthcare—I realize how fortunate and wealthy I really am.

I found that as I demonstrated gratitude for the financial resources that I have, more money came my way in the form of yearly salary raises, a job promotion, and grant money to pay down my student loan debt. Also, being thankful for what I have has resulted in a spirit of contentment with a clear focus on knowing what matters most to me: my family and friends. Money certainly can't buy that.

How you think about your ability to live on a public interest attorney's salary will determine whether you succeed at living prosperously on a modest income. Until I had gained control over my money, I thought that the ability to live nicely was based on how much money you made. Ultimately, I learned that this is not true. It really has a lot to do with how you manage what you make. Your ability to successfully manage your money has a lot to do with your attitude. If you believe you can thrive on a public interest attorney's salary, you can. If you don't believe you can, you most likely won't. If you are in the latter category, applying the principles and strategies that I have shown throughout this book may just change your mind.

I do not know your present financial situation. However, I can probably guess that your financial problems did not crop up overnight. Therefore, don't expect them to be solved that way. This is a journey that you will enjoy as you certainly will start to see progress and improvement in your finances.

I can't repeat this enough: there will be times when you will want to give up—don't. Things will happen that will derail or stall your financial progress. When that occurs, just regroup and press on. Each hurdle that you overcome will make you stronger. Be grateful that you have income to get you back on your feet.

I deal with obstacles by writing down three things for which I am grateful. Oftentimes, I think back on how far I have come in handling my money that now, when I am faced with a financial challenge, I hardly even sweat it because I usually have enough money to cover it. When I'm short on funds, I revise my Spending Plan to cover the difference. During those times when my emergency account was at its lowest, I was thankful and took comfort knowing that I am not completely broke because I have a nicely funded 401(k) retirement account.

When it comes to my salary as a public interest attorney, I do not whine and throw a pity party. In fact, because of what I have achieved financially, I am not intimidated around private attorneys, or any other professional for that matter, who may earn more money than I do. My financial habits are creating real long-lasting wealth for me. Because I am content with where I currently am with my finances, I am not susceptible to get-rich-quick schemes. I see that my money plan is working, and I am having a blast in the process.

Regardless of your salary, the only person who is stopping you from moving forward is you. Make the decision right now that you will not use your salary as a public interest attorney as an excuse for not living your best life. If tackling your student loan debt seems daunting right now, then start saving your change and applying it toward a short-term financial goal to give you a boost and get you going. The key is to do *something* and to take it one step at a time.

For those of you who are considering working in the area of public interest law and want to advocate for those who are less fortunate, I hope that this book has convinced you that you can work for a legal services organization and still prosper financially. There is such a great need for competent and caring lawyers to help those who are often overlooked and disregarded—the poor. You can't put a price tag on the fulfillment that comes from this kind of work. I am grateful each day for the opportunity to make a meaningful difference in the lives of all the clients I serve.

Finally, what I would like to say to my fellow legal aid colleagues throughout the country who work tirelessly on behalf of the poor is to hang in there. Apply the techniques in this book for financial success that I've utilized. Not only will you reap personal satisfaction but financial satisfaction as well.

CPSIA information can be obtained at www.ICGtesting.com
Printed in the USA
BVOW032103110213

312974BV00002B/16/P

9 781441 511409